W9-APN-575

Basic Research in Finance

Needs and Prospects

Basic Research in Finance
Needs and Prospects

Edited by

Charles C. Abbott

Published by the Graduate School of Business Administration
University of Virginia
Distributed by the University Press of Virginia
Charlottesville

Preface

THE need for basic research in commercial and investment banking, to say nothing of other types of financial institutions, is pinpointed by the fact that both groups of bankers are deeply concerned whether or not their clients have research and development divisions.

Starting some thirty-seven years ago on the premise that banking should do basic research in its own field, efforts have been made to interest both individual banks and banking associations in such a program. Strangely enough, despite arguments, speeches, and a series of articles, no interested response has been forthcoming, although in other parts of the financial world, notably in the insurance industry, considerable research has been undertaken. Bankers' associations claim to have active research departments, and certainly some individual banks do have. But analysis shows that most of the research referred to is usually called "market research," based on the collation and study of statistics in the general field of business.

It has been difficult to give practical men in the financial world a clear idea of what is meant by basic research as opposed to statistical research or market research. The question usually involves, "What do you expect to find through basic research, and, when found, what will you do with the results?" The answer is obvious. "If what one is looking for is already known and if what is to be done is already decided, there is no point in research."

Because of past failure to persuade banks and bank associations to undertake the basic research which they themselves require of their best and largest customers, Dr. Charles C. Abbott, Dean of the University of Virginia Graduate School of Business Administration, was approached to help find a solution to this problem.

As a consequence, this collection of memoranda and extracts from letters has been arranged, under the Dean's stimulus and guidance, pointing up the need for basic research in the whole financial field, including the banking industry, to the end that the financial community may rethink its position, responsibilities, and opportunities. Dean Abbott has grouped the articles in five sections and has prepared commentaries on each section. This symposium is published in the hope that it will precipitate some effort in the direction of basic research in this area of the United States' economy.

Many students of the subject believe that, unless the financial world undertakes a wide-ranging but coordinated program of basic research, both commercial and investment banking houses in their traditional forms can and conceivably will be superseded by mutual institutions whose operations border on the socialization of credit. If that is not the outcome of the failure of private institutions to assume this research responsibility, the gap may be filled by an extension of governmental activities. As is well known, the government has already made great headway in occupying economic areas that could have been, or still can be, preserved for private enterprise.

THOMAS C. BOUSHALL
Richmond, Virginia
October 1965

Acknowledgments

GRATEFUL acknowledgment is made to the Life Insurance Association of America and to the *Journal of Finance* for permission to reprint condensations of their publications. Appendix A, "The Investment Research Program of the Life Insurance Business," is condensed from *1964 Record of Life Insurance Investments,* a report to the members of the Life Insurance Association by James J. O'Leary. Appendix B, "Research in the Capital Markets," is condensed from a report with the same title by the National Bureau Exploratory Committee on Research in the Capital Markets, which appeared as a supplement to the *Journal of Finance,* Vol. XIX (May 1964), No. 2, Part 2.

Permissions to quote are gratefully acknowledged as follows: The *Journal of Finance* for excerpts from "Application of Flow-of-Funds to Interest-Rate Forecasting," by William C. Freund and Edward D. Zinbarg, in its March 1965 issue, and from "An Exposition of the Structure of the Flow-of-Funds Accounts," by Lawrence S. Ritter, in its May 1963 issue.

Syracuse University Press for a passage from the introduction to *The Silent Partners: Institutional Investors and Corporate Control,* by Daniel Baum and Ned B. Stiles (Syracuse, N. Y., 1965).

The editor also wishes to thank John Barnett, Nancy D'Agostino, Banner Bruton, Ann Devening, Gloria Newbold, and Tommie Sue Reed, for their assistance in preparing the manuscript of this symposium.

C. C. A.

Contents

Introduction

The Why-How-What of This Symposium

THE following letter, mailed in July 1965, to fewer than fifty persons, initiated this symposium:

> We, the undersigned, are concerned – in fact, for some time we have been concerned – with what we consider a lack of basic research as distinct from applied research in the field of finance, particularly as regards the role of financial institutions, including commercial banks and security houses. By basic research we mean research and speculative thinking undertaken not with reference to immediate profit, present practice or the existing structure of the financial world, but initiated with reference to the services and functions the financial world might or should perform for the public generally and the whole economy, particularly the private sector. We are also interested in what the behavior and characteristics of financial institutions and the private financial world should be if they are to act as an effective check on the expansion of the public sector.
>
> Our concern is the more acute because we feel financial institutions and the financial world for some years have been going through a great transformation, both structurally and functionally, and that the end is by no means in sight.
>
> We do not know how widely our feeling may be shared and this is one reason for this letter. It is being sent to the persons listed on the attached sheet.
>
> A further reason for this letter is that each of the undersigned has undertaken to prepare a short five–ten page memorandum indicating the areas of basic research in the financial world he personally thinks

should be explored at this time and the reasons therefor.

We are asking each person to whom this letter is addressed if he would be willing to prepare a similar memorandum for informal circulation among the group. Those who cooperate in the undertaking will receive copies of all the memoranda. Hopefully we will have all of the memoranda in hand by September 1, 1965.

Until we see what the response is to this letter we obviously cannot plan a further step. However, if these memoranda should develop some common areas of concern or establish rough boundaries for a field meriting exploration, this in itself might point in the direction of further action – for example more systematic research, a series of lectures, seminars or some other type of effort. As a minimum we think these memoranda collectively may be a most stimulating symposium.

If you should be interested in this undertaking, kindly communicate with Dean Abbott at the Graduate School of Business Administration, University of Virginia.

Sincerely,

Charles C. Abbott
Dean, Graduate School
of Business Administration
University of Virginia

James K. Hart
Executive Vice President
The Lehman Corporation

Thomas C. Boushall
Chairman of the Board
Bank of Virginia

Charles B. Harding
Retired Chairman of the
Board
Smith, Barney & Company

Ora C. Roehl
Financial and Management Consultant
Boston, Massachusetts

By design this letter did not define "basic research" with great precision and left somewhat ambiguous how this concept was to be differentiated from "applied research." The thought was that the results of the inquiry would be more fruitful if each respondent was left free to choose his own definition.

In effect the letter asked two questions: First, did the recipients of the letter share the belief of its signers that the present quantity and quality of basic financial research were inadequate? Secondly, if this feeling was shared, were there common areas of concern? Could a consensus perhaps be achieved, even if only modest, as to the subject areas that needed exploration?

The response to the letter seems to have answered the first question definitively and affirmatively. Fewer than fifty letters were sent out. Replies were received from some three-fourths of the recipients. Virtually all the respondents, even those who for one reason or another could not contribute to the symposium, indicated concern – about all kinds of things. A number of persons not originally approached heard of the letter and wrote to indicate their interest.

Several replies recognized the substantial amount of solid work carried out during the past decade by a variety of foundations, industries, universities, research organizations, and individual persons and published in periodicals, as monographs, and in other ways. Nevertheless, the need for additional research and, particularly, of a new viewpoint and a fresh approach was a recurring theme. For example, Ora C. Roehl's memorandum states:

> In the financial world solid basic research is still very much in the developing stage. Research in the financial field is still too much concerned with the rationalization of the *status quo*, and a rationalization effort is not research. It is rather an effort to defend existing conditions, whether they are good or bad, and it is the antithesis of the search for truth. Many financial institutions have set up research departments, but they are generally oriented to market research, although some do get into technological developments concerned with computers and other means to facilitate mechanical operations.

Other respondents make similar observations, and W. Giles Mellon points out:

> This [recent] research has, in the main, been directed toward explanation and prediction of the existing financial system. . . .
>
> What Messrs. Abbott, Boushall, Harding, Hart, and Roehl are proposing is an extension in research on optimal behavior to include the financial system as a whole. . . .
>
> There is little doubt that such a program of research would be valuable and would fill a real need in the financial area – if it can be carried out in an effective manner.

Similarly Donald B. Woodward writes:

> At no time, so far as I am aware, have the financial institutions comprising the financial system done any research to analyze the total function of the system as related to the total economy and the individuals in that economy. Nor have other groups, so far as I know, gone far in such an effort.

Commonly the wish both for more work and for work of a different type was supported by one or another of the following concepts: a recognition that a public responsibility adheres to much if not all the operations of financial institutions; a realization that the financial structure and financial practices are in the midst of a period of great change; a suspicion that some of our accepted analytical techniques are inadequate for the rapidly evolving situation; an implicit or explicit acknowledgment that in the financial world, as elsewhere, research is intimately related to leadership.

The answer to the second question in the letter was less clear. If the collection of memoranda and extracts from letters is read carefully, certain questions and problems recur. There is, in fact, some grouping or clustering of thoughts and ideas as to problem areas that particularly need attention. On the other hand, perhaps the most striking characteristic of the collection is the wide range of topics mentioned, the scope of the symposium as a whole, and the heterogeneity of matters discussed –

a heterogeneity so great as to be extraordinary. For example, contributions placed in Part II, "Appraising the Changing Structure, Functions, and Services of the Financial World," deal with the entire financial structure – including institutions, financial practices, the flow of funds, the relation of the public and private sectors, and public policy – and explicitly or implicitly present an extremely large and variegated array of topics about which we know too little. Other contributors deal, more intensively, with areas that may be smaller but are of critical importance. Ralph F. Leach, for example, restricts – if that word can be used appropriately here – his suggestions "primarily to the government securities market, with particular reference to the viability of that market under the changed ground rules since 1961." Ezra Solomon shrewdly concentrates on the importance, both for capital markets and the economy at large, of a better understanding of the cost-of-capital concept. Bion B. Howard entitles his memorandum "The Declining Role of the Investment Banker in Corporation Finance." Robert G. Kirby deals specifically with the growing responsibilities of financial intermediaries:

> To date the financial intermediary has accepted only the research responsibility. ... A much broader responsibility exists somewhere in this complex that no one has yet been willing to accept. The magnitude of this responsibility seems likely to grow substantially with the passage of time.

In an effort to give the symposium some degree of order and unity and make it more meaningful, the contributions have been arranged under a number of headings, each part prefaced by some slight editorial comment and explanation. Needless to say, the groupings and the part headings evolved from study of the contributions; they are not determined *ex ante*. Some general observations about the collection as a whole, however, and the way it should be regarded may help to place it in perspective.

These memoranda and extracts in no sense represent a scientific sample of thought and belief. Nor are they the result of systematic research directed at a predetermined end or designed to test any hypothesis. What we have here is simply a canvass of opinion. The commentaries, however, are those of competent, experienced, and knowledgeable men. The views come from a number of geographical areas and a variety of institutions – commercial banks, insurance companies, security houses, mutual funds – as well as from the academic world and financial press. The contributors wrote as they did, memoranda or letters, wholly independently of each other, each drawing on his own background and experience. The late Wallace B. Donham, when Dean of the Harvard Business School, used to say that informed gossip ought never to be disregarded; neither should informed opinion.

Most readers, I believe, will be struck by the thoughtful tone of the collection, by the concern for the public good, and by the sense of public responsibility. Frequently asked, though posed in different ways, are three closely related questions: Is the present structure of financial institutions, is the range of services they purvey, is the framework of regulation within which they operate, in fact well designed to accomplish national purposes, however these may be defined?

Similarly I think many persons will sense a kind of power running through a majority of the contributions. This is not the type of power that emanates from long-continued scholarship conscientiously applied or from an elegant theoretical exposition. On the contrary, it is the distinctive feel of strength that adheres to writing done by men who for a long time have lived close to and are thoroughly familiar with the portions of reality they are describing and analyzing and who have thought intensively about these combinations of institutions, men, knowledge, and practices.

In a large fraction of this collection can be discerned the underlying thought that one of the things most needed is an assessment of existing information, an appraisal of where we are. Charles Moeller, Jr., for example, states: "In the area of fuller utilization of existing knowledge and data, new fields for research seem especially bright." W. Giles Mellon suggests that "a logical first point of departure would be to sponsor a project to survey all extant research in the financial area which is relevant to the question of how the financial system might be reformed," and Samuel B. Chase, Jr., adds: "There does not exist a formal theoretical framework for evaluating the performance of financial institutions comparable to the framework used in economic studies of, say, the performance of manufacturing industries." Robert F. Vandell states: "My first interest is in seeing that we make the most of research currently in progress. . . .The record is not good."

What lies behind this line of thinking seemingly is a desire for careful consideration and reconsideration of known data, of existing institutions, practice, and regulation, and – particularly – of the implications of the present situation for five, ten, or twenty years ahead. Contemplative thinking of this type is not, by and large, characteristic of the financial world nor, in many cases, of large-scale institutionalized research. It is, however, peculiarly the province of the individual scholar.

This stress on determining where we are now and on reexamination of the present scene does not mean that further investigations are not desired. Indeed, quite the contrary. The number and quality of suggestions that the symposium has brought together are in fact remarkable; and for researchers the stimulation afforded by these ideas may well be the greatest use of this book.

Two notes that recur a number of times are the desire for a more careful consideration of the needs of customers of financial institutions and the wish for a more refined flow-of-funds analysis in view of the large and increasing role of financial intermediaries in the economy. Half a dozen authors mention the importance of more thorough and more comprehensive flow-of-funds analyses, and C. Stewart Sheppard and Carlton R. Copp devote their memoranda to this topic. Sheppard emphasizes this:

> Apart from the continuing challenge of constructing a macro-economic model of the functioning of the total economy through integration of product and income accounts, input-output analysis, and flow of funds, there exist specific challenges to relate flow of funds to corporate sources and uses of funds, to business fluctuations, and to interest rate forecasting.

Copp relates the sources-and-uses-of-funds concept to the existing structure of financial intermediaries and their relative efficiencies:

> An examination of the potential *sources* of funds for the national economy could be made. It would be interesting to see whether there will be sufficient savings. . .to provide for. . .demands – or whether the government will have greatly to extend the credit base artificially to meet its long-term goals.

> .   .   .   .   .

> Using this framework of the sources and uses of short-term and investment funds, it would then be possible to measure the *relative cost effectiveness* of various financial institutions.

The flow-of-funds analysis acquires a particular cogency in view of the great growth of financial intermediaries during the last generation. Indeed, the whole question of these intermediaries – their function, future role, responsibilities, and place in flow-of-funds analysis – was of such interest to a number of participants that a special section in the symposium has been set aside for those contributions specially concerned with this range of subjects.

One final point merits special mention. While many of the ideas tossed in the air in this collection are, perhaps, subject to objective analysis, many are not. Throughout the symposium questions and considerations are posed whose determination requires, on the one hand, clarity regarding basic assumptions and, on the other, subjective values and value judgments. One example is the query raised by Joseph A. Livingston:

> I have wondered for a long time whether the vast effort that goes into the distribution of private capital is justified. I refer specifically to the elaborate Wall Street apparatus – the daily trading on the New York Stock Exchange in stocks and bonds – requiring thousands of brokerage firms and many more thousands of floor broker and telephone traders.

> The mere question challenges assumptions we have all been brought up on – the liquidity of the market place.

Such problems are not easily "quantified"; nor are they likely to be resolved solely in terms of objective statistical analysis.

The diversity of the contributions to this collection has made peculiarly difficult the task of arranging them in – hopefully – a somewhat orderly manner. Needless to say, the headings selected for the several parts and the placement of particular contributions in one group or another are necessarily arbitrary and far from perfect. Numerous items could have been placed in sections other than the ones where they are; certainly material dealt with in one segment often overlaps that dealt with in others. Nevertheless it is believed that an arrangement of *some* sort, no matter how imperfect and capricious, may be of help to readers. If the headings selected or the arrangement of the items offends either the sense of orderliness of readers or the sensibilities of authors, I can only offer sincere apologies. Needless to say, the contributions themselves have been edited only in the interest of consistent format. While some smoothing and collating of the items might, perhaps, have resulted in a more uniform result, such an effort would have been wholly illegitimate. Furthermore, an attempt of this sort would inevitably have altered the character and flavor of the collection and its sense of reality, which are, perhaps, among its greatest virtues.

In conclusion I wish to say that if the contributors to this symposium feel individually that the ideas and points of views represented in the collection are sufficiently interesting and provocative to reward them for the time and effort they expended in making their contributions, then one of the major purposes of this effort will have been accomplished – and we all will have benefited.

CHARLES C. ABBOTT
Charlottesville, Virginia
December 1965

PART I

Research and Leadership

Commentary

IN THE United States in the twentieth century it is common-
place to equate "research" with "leadership" – in medicine, education, aerospace, manufacturing, and a host of technical
fields. As Thomas C. Boushall points out in his memorandum:
"Basic research in industry has been an essential insurance
against obsolescence."

The memoranda here grouped under "Research and Leadership" have two recurring themes: that the financial world during
the last generation or two has not engaged extensively in basic
research and that it has not provided the leadership that could
have been expected from it in view of its importance in the economy or, indeed, that was needed in its own self-interest. The
suggestion is that a casual relationship has existed.

Donald B. Woodward points out: "Much of the progressive
improvement in the financial system over the years has come
from sources external to it and has not been generated by it."
Samuel B. Chase, Jr., states: "Innovation, so prized in the
manufacturing sector, is often viewed with suspicion in finance" – and admittedly innovation is one of the prime goals of
research. Thomas C. Boushall adds: "It is reasonable to believe that if banking had engaged in basic research thirty to
forty years ago . . . , there would not have been the need or opportunity for many competitive and restrictive services to be
inaugurated or their growth encouraged and accelerated."
Maurice Nelles, writing from outside the financial world, says:
"It has been my observation that, as far as finance is concerned, research has been of the 'data-gathering and correlation' type. This type of research is very important, but it is
primarily historical and only projections from it can be important."

In his paper Howard C. Tharsing relates "leadership" to
standards of behavior and integrity, to the position of the

private sector of the financial world vis-à-vis the public sector, and to the role of the financial intermediary. It would, perhaps, have been proper to place this contribution in the final part of the symposium, which is specifically concerned with financial intermediaries, but the connotations that Tharsing attaches to "leadership," which are somewhat different from those of the other contributors to that section, seem to justify placing it here. He says:

> A research project considering the ethical code of of the financial community should not develop a code of practice . . . and probably could not. . . . Rather it would review the development of the present code. . . . The right project in this area might enable the financial community to assume leadership in a field of increasing public concern. . . . Leadership in this area could be useful in checking the expansion of the public sector.

Collectively these memoranda suggest that two primary consequences have followed from this lack of self-examination on the part of financial institutions and from this absence of voluntarily enforced standards of behavior, or self-regulation. First, study of the financial system has come primarily from outside – from governmental regulatory bodies, from politicians, from the academic world. Second, it has been primarily these forces that have either introduced innovations in financial practice or have encouraged the growth of new and competitive financial institutions. The validity of these conclusions is supported by memoranda included in subsequent sections of the symposium.

Even if true, such developments need not be deemed necessarily and entirely bad – though this may depend on the point of view. More significant, perhaps, is another thought that recurs also in the next grouping in this collection, "Appraising the Changing Structure, Functions, and Services of the Financial World." This line of thinking is to the effect that neither the financial world itself nor the "outside" innovators who have introduced changes have supplied a theoretical framework by which to judge, on the one hand, the efficiency of the financial world's operations or, on the other hand, the over-all social utility of the individual regulations within which financial operations take place.

If this line of thinking is accepted as having some validity, its implications are not confined to the field of finance; they extend throughout the entire economic structure.

Memorandum

Donald B. Woodward
Managing Partner
A. W. Jones & Company

WE LIVE in a money economy. Both the functioning of the total economy and the satisfactions of the individuals comprising it depend importantly upon the performance of the intermediary institutions which make up the financial system. On the over-all record, these intermediary institutions have done a commendable job: we have an impressive economy, and progressive improvement has been sizable over decades.

But three additional observations may also, I think, be fairly made:

1. Much of the progressive improvement in the financial system over the years has come from sources external to it and has not been generated by it, e.g., the FRS, deposit and share insurance, information disclosure to investors, cash values and grace periods in life insurance, IBRD, and IMF.

2. Compared with industry's research and development budget of billions of dollars a year, the financial system, I believe, spends relatively little – though it has supported generously some good studies. But the major research work in the financial area has been done by government, universities, and foundations.

3. At no time, so far as I am aware, have the financial institutions comprising the financial system done any research to analyze the total function of the system as related to the total economy and the individuals in that economy. Nor have other groups, so far as I know, gone far in such an effort. The result is that the preponderant part of such work as has been done has pertained only to individual parts of the financial system.

Paragraphs 2 and 3 suggest that a major analytical inquiry into the functioning of the total financial system in its relationship to the functioning of the economy and the satisfaction of individuals ought to serve a useful purpose and identify possible improvements for the benefit of all.

What are some of the studies that would be involved in such a major project? I submit ten below, with no effort to indicate order of importance.

I. The Family.

What are the needs of families in various groups for all kinds of financial services, and how may they best be provided? What financial needs may families of various types reasonably anticipate over time and how may they best make provision for these needs? Should more attention be given to lifetime budgeting? Would families be better served by alternatives to disorganized dealing with many different kinds of financial institutions?

II. Size of Institutions

What are the economics of institutional size and variety of service, with due consideration for present technologies? We see Metropolitan Life and the Bank of America, for example, alongside the country bank, the tiny life insurance company, and the tiny savings and loan company. We see some institutions offering a variety of financial services – though none provide a full department store range. Can we lay aside deep traditional prejudices and study cost and efficiency?

III. Experience

What can experience teach of possible improvement in lending and investment? Important work has been done on loss ratios of some types of instruments and equities, but little on others. What are the best criteria? It is my impression that most is known about bonds and mortgages, least about corporate equities and various kinds of loans. Financial institutions are full of data, largely unanalyzed.

IV. Business and Employment

What is the relationship between the functioning of the whole financial system and prosperity, growth, and employment? The focus of most work on this subject has been currency and bank deposits, and, more lately, the fisc. How valid are our conflicting views, and how good is the evidence on which they are based?

V. Community Planning

The growth and development of communities – rural and urban – deeply concern financial institutions and are the source of much loss both socially and financially. The financial system has much knowledge and a vast store of data on this subject. More extensive analysis would surely produce information to curtail at least some of the social and financial loss and tragedy.

VI. Morality

Financial intermediaries have extensive interest in and contact with the morality and integrity of the business and the general population. Much attention is given to these characteristics. They are important factors in cost, loss, sources of funds, joy, and tragedy. Would a careful and major study of these moral qualities provide significant information in the interests of all?

VII. World Development

The financial system of the United States is a very important factor in world development – in the fate of other peoples, both those well developed and those less so, and hence in world tensions resulting in war or peace. A few financial institutions give marked attention to the subject; most, and the system itself, give very little – and some none at all. Major exploration of the possibilities would be in the interest of everyone.

VIII. Change

The financial system has been tremendously affected by change, which is a marked feature of our time. Change is likely to be a feature for years to come, judging by the vast number of people and resources now devoted to the production of change. An organized and comprehensive study of the prospects for future change, based on present-day knowledge, plans, and research, would seem to be in the interest of financial institutions, their clientele, and the public.

IX. *People*

Financial institutions are operated by and for people. Both the successes and the failures of people are of vital interest to these institutions. What motivates people to do what, what brings them to success, what causes personal problems that become financial and social problems? The most intensive and extensive study is needed.

X. *Legal Framework*

Financial institutions are confined in a legal framework, much of which grew like Topsy, and some of which in relation to present and future conditions has the rationale of the dodo. The studies here proposed would probably point to legal problems in several directions. A forthright study of the legal framework seems desirable.

The suggestions made above are based on the following propositions: (a) Financial intermediaries have greater responsibilities to themselves and their clientele than they have yet faced; they occupy a position something like that of the United States in world affairs, (b) They need to take the past and the future more seriously and to mobilize all the information they have and can get, (c) They ought to organize a research program big enough to cope with the need. Probably it ought to amount to something like $50 million to $100 million a year for ten years.

The studies I think urgent I have given only in thumbnail sketches; each could be elaborated if agreed upon – and this elaboration would be a project in itself.

Basic Research Needs
in Financial Economics

Samuel B. Chase, Jr.
Senior Staff
The Brookings Institution

BASIC research is indeed needed on questions relating to the
adequacy of present financial institutions and arrangements to
meet present needs and, even more importantly, to provide
the flexibility required if financial markets are to play their
proper role in future economic progress. The greatest dangers, it would seem, rest in the possibility that an outmoded
system of financial regulation will stand in the way of needed
innovation and general adaptation to new circumstances.

In the finance industry, public policy, including both legislation and administrative regulation, is aimed not so much at
fostering competition as at regulating, controlling, and manipu-
lating it. Regulation is pervasive, and a basic underlying premise of most of it is that free competition is inimical to the
social good. Innovation, so prized in the manufacturing sector, is often viewed with suspicion in finance. The "public
utility" approach to the finance industry has grown out of sad
experience. The need for a stable system of financial institutions which can be relied on to meet fiduciary responsibilities
is clear.

But what are the proper guidelines for government intervention? The methods of control that have been adopted in this
country are specific products of specific circumstances, not
the result of a careful analysis of the shortcomings of unregulated private financial enterprise. They were often developed
under conditions of emergency, and they lack a cohesive rationale. If these methods of control interfere with the efficient
allocation of credit and stifle desirable financial innovation,

they foster increased government action to fill "credit gaps" and in general to meet needs not met by the private sector.

Recent successes of fiscal and monetary policies cast doubt on the rationale of much regulation aimed at insuring stability. It would appear that as monetary and fiscal policies have become increasingly potent forces working for economic stability, the need for sacrificing competition among financial institutions for the sake of stability is reduced.

Guidelines in this area require an understanding of the role of financial institutions in the saving-investment process and in particular an understanding of the contribution of these institutions to economic well-being and progress. There is no theory of finance capable of providing this guidance. That is, there does not exist a formal theoretical framework for evaluating the performance of financial institutions comparable to the framework used in economic studies of, say, the performance of manufacturing industries.

Lack of a comprehensive theory that explains why financial markets and institutions come into being, and how they relate to the performance of the economy, severely impedes the progress of research and policy formation in many areas. Recent applications of the theory of portfolio analysis to financial markets have provided the starting point for development of a comprehensive theory of finance along the lines pioneered by Gurley and Shaw. Further basic research along these lines seems indispensable if we are to pinpoint the virtues and dangers of unregulated competition. Progress at the theoretical level will facilitate systematic analysis of a broad range of issues. Some specific questions in point are listed below. The list is intended to be illustrative not exhaustive.

I. Enforced Specialization of Financial Institutions

To what extent is it desirable to limit the scope of private financial institutions? Today financial intermediaries, including banks, are closely restricted in the kinds of liabilities they can issue and the kinds of assets they can hold. These restrictions may stand in the way of efficiency and innovation and may even lead to the kinds of instability they are presumably designed to prevent.

II. The Firm in Finance

What are the proper structure and function of financial firms? There has been a growing interest in applying the economic theory of the firm to financial businesses. At the level of pure theory many obstacles are encountered. It is not easy to define and measure the product of a financial firm. This in turn makes difficult the application of concepts of efficiency in production. Considerations relating to uncertainty and risk present another important obstacle to formulating research on the performance of financial institutions.

Beyond these problems of theory, on which considerable research is needed, lie questions of structure and performance of alternative forms of organization. The emerging interest in academic circles in the problems of bank merger and branch banking coincides with a critical juncture at which the Congress is deciding whether or not antitrust laws apply to commercial banking. The conflict between the philosophy of antitrust and the general philosophy of financial regulation is enormous. Economic research ought to be able to contribute materially to an understanding of the social implications of alternative approaches to these questions.

Another related problem is that of appraising the role of mutuals. In the savings field, corporations, such as commercial banks and some savings and loan associations, compete alongside mutual savings and loans and mutual savings banks. We know very little about the differences between the two forms of organization and the motives that guide mutuals as opposed to those that guide corporations. Not much formal work has been done on this important problem.

III. The Role of Deposit and Related Insurance

Deposit insurance and federal insurance of share capital of savings and loan associations doubtless have great virtue. But they have become sacred cows. Clearly, the federal government must be interested in the management of institutions whose liabilities it insures. But there is a danger that the system is too inflexible. It has often been asserted by academic economists that insured institutions should be free to pursue more venturesome policies, provided that their premiums rise to reflect added risk to the government. The idea deserves intensive exploration. So far the technicians have contended that such an approach is infeasible, but observation of private insurance companies and their practices suggests that it is not.

IV. Government Lending and Insurance of Private Debt

Government loan insurance has produced remarkable results, especially in housing. Direct government loan programs have done likewise. These kinds of intervention are often defended on the ground that they fill "credit gaps" that a really efficient private credit market would ideally take care of. Are these assertions true? If so, why does the private market fail to meet legitimate credit needs? If the market works unsatisfactorily, what criteria can be developed to choose among alternative forms of intervention?

Statement on the Essential Need for Basic Research in Banking and Finance

Thomas C. Boushall
Chairman of the Board
The Bank of Virginia

THE acceleration of knowledge in industry, the services, medicine, and the multiple technical sciences has been generally the product of basic research and consequent applied research. The abbreviated expression "R & D" has become a part of the language of the day. Unless this symbol appears in reports of organizations and institutions, those organizations and institutions are considered to be out of the main stream of present American progress. The reported expenditure in government and private endeavor of some $100 billion a year on some form of research reflects the emphasis of leaders and thinkers on America's need to keep abreast or in the lead of world effort and progress today.

It is depressing to find no thinking or awareness, and certainly no acceptance and action, in this whole area of activity on the part of the management of the banking structure and the finance corporations, the members of financial firms and partnerships. Search has not yet unearthed any evidence of such activity. In fact, inquiry results in a response that basic research is no part of the banking activity, either individual, institutional, or associational, nor in the area of the multiple finance services.

Through examination and inquiry it develops that among bankers the term "research" connotes primarily the accumulation, interpretation, and projection into the future of statistics, much as one would tabulate the total number of tons of steel produced in past years and then project the figures on into the years ahead on a trend line. Sometimes the line may be adjusted to show projected or expected production of automobiles or other objects using steel.

The steel companies, however, are doing basic research, related to the nature and quality of their product, with the hope and prospect that some heretofore unknown and unvisualized product or procedure or combination thereof may further perfect the product or find new uses for it. Once such a breakthrough occurs, then research is conducted on how the new discovery may be applied to the company's processes for a more profitable operation.

Research and development in banking is a search for guidelines from past experience, a search into competitive financial facilities, a search for new services. But it is not a search for basic things that could arise out of purely objective studies with no specified goals other than a search for the now unknown, which, when discovered, might then be studied for practical application.

All of this applies equally to the various fields of financial service.

It is reasonable to believe that if banking had engaged in basic research thirty to forty years ago when basic research was not widely undertaken in such fields as medicine and metallurgy, wood products and coal, and electricity and electric services – research such as AT&T has long carried on – there would not have been the need or opportunity for many competitive and restrictive services to be inaugurated or their growth encouraged and accelerated. For example, real down-to-earth research could have eliminated the rapid development under federal aegis and encouragement of the following services: savings and loan associations, credit unions, federal agricultural credit corporations, federal guarantees of bank deposits, and federal guarantees of home improvement loans and mortgage loans. The many restrictions and limitations on banking organization processes and on the spread of banking structures need not have occurred. Nor would there have been so great an invasion of the financial services that banks could have developed and safely and soundly performed – services now largely handled by insurance companies in the term-loan field, the mortgage-loan field, and the pension and annuity area. In fact, many services in the investment field (not including the services of brokerage houses operating on the several stock exchanges) could have been performed by banks. I refer to such services as are now rendered by the investment trust organizations.

Basic research by these financial agencies could have afforded greater growth to them, greater protection to the general public, and greater opportunity for accelerated development of many of the service organizations and of the production and distribution of heavy and light manufactured products. For an example of the beneficial efforts of research let us turn to the public utilities. Through their basic research the price of electricity to the public has remained practically static over four decades despite the rise in wages, cost of fuel and equipment, and taxes. Banking and finance have no such parallel to present.

While the legal rate of allowable interest has not been greatly changed on large loans, laws and practice have permitted double or triple rates when loans are made to an individual on a monthly repayment basis, or when paper arising out of merchant sales or long-term purchase contracts is purchased.

Proof of the failure of banks to serve the public adequately in the field of personal borrowing is the vast proliferation of personal loan companies with legalized interest rates that run from 24 per cent to 42 per cent a year. It has been said that 90 per cent of the borrowers from small loan services would be readily eligible for loans from banks' personal loan departments.

The present bureaucratic supervision of financial services on a narrow, permissive basis can be presumed to stem in large measure from the absence of basic research in areas where it could not only identify, and seek voluntary correction of, abuses, but could so basically structure the rendering of self-policed services as not to require or warrant government or public supervision. Our basic American principle of faith is free enterprise – enterprise free of the bureaucratic control common in Europe and under totalitarian governments. Yet we fail in our conduct of the free enterprise system by permitting abuses that result in a demand for public protection through government supervision and the restriction of our freedom.

Basic research in banking and finance could be an important contribution and a prime example of leadership in the development of the resources of our land and of our people.

Today government officers and congressional and legislative representatives are conceiving and implementing our financial tax structures and are converting a goodly part of the people's salaries and wages into socialized services rendered through government agencies. They are the leaders in our economic and social developments through political action. It is hard to find fault with the bureaucrat or the politician who, sensing public needs with respect to health, education, medical care, pensions, availability of home-purchasing power, crop loans and controls, small business credits, urban renewal and re-development, and reduction of poverty, sets out to meet the problems and thus endears himself and his party to the voters.

Of course, basic research in banking and finance could not produce solutions for all the problems that have developed in our rapidly expanding society and economy. But it is possible that sustained research over the past thirty years could have found and developed fundamentals that could have stemmed from and been included in the private enterprise system – that could have furnished sound programs that would either have eliminated the unfilled needs or have reduced them to a point where governmental participation would have been minimal instead of maximal.

The issue presented here is illustrated by the lack of re-search to pinpoint the abuses developed in our free enterprise operation – abuses that brought governmental supervision and restraint – and by the development of vacuums in areas of public needs. These vacuums an affluent society could have filled by concerted private understanding and effort instead of leaving them for the government to pre-empt by means of services financed out of the earnings of the people and corporations by way of enforced taxation. And this taxation must cover also the cost of an inefficient and profligate bureaucracy.

The real issue is this: In spite of the all-but-miraculous results of basic research in the industries and sciences and the consequent affluent society we here in the United States have achieved, banking and finance have not been willing and eager handmaidens in serving these developments. In and of themselves banking and finance have made no original contributions to the functioning of our society through basic research in the financial field. Instead of researching and developing ways and means of channeling the rising incomes of corporations and individuals into agencies of service to the general public within the framework of free enterprise, the financial community neglected research and consequently remained unaware of the growing needs and the vacuums, which thus became "red meat" to political parties and politicians.

Is not the startling penetration of government agencies and functions into an area that could, in large measure, have been reserved to private enterprise sufficient warning that we in banking and finance must be up and doing? Must we not seek first to parallel the great successes of industry and science in the field of basic research and, second, to preserve the all-too-small area remaining to private enterprise activities?

How shall we proceed if we are persuaded that such an effort should be organized? Power companies and industry carry on their basic research in individual companies and secure patent protection on their developments. But in banking and finance there is no product to protect. Once a new concept or service is developed, it promptly becomes the common property of the industry. Hence it would seem that associational effort is logical for the establishment and development of basic research in banking and finance. It would seem wise to locate such a program on a university campus, where professors, libraries, and student assistants would be available. But it would also seem wise to seek out some experienced personnel from banking and finance fields; they might be a helpful contribution to the search for the unknown and the early recognition of the adaptability of such findings to the fields supporting the effort.

Basic research in industry has been an essential insurance against obsolescence and a bid for a stake in the future of a dynamic economy such as ours in America. The field in which banking and finance operate has been far more deeply penetrated by government agencies than has the field of industry and commercial services. Basic research exists in the less-penetrated field; it does not exist in the more-penetrated field. The need for insurance against the obsolescence of private enterprise and against the predominance of government agencies is imperative. The need for the financial system to make a bid for a continuing and enlarging stake in the future is equally demanding.

Extract from Letter

Maurice Nelles
Manufacturing Research & Development
Westinghouse Defense Center

AS YOU KNOW, I have been in research for many years and in many fields. It has been my observation that, as far as finance is concerned, research has been of the "data-gathering and correlation" type. This type of research is very important, but it is primarily historical and only projections from it can be important.

This fact may give a clue as to how to proceed. That is, exclude the data-gathering type of research and start studies in areas which are of interest. The example which first comes to mind would be: "What arrangement could be substituted for financial institutions such as Lehman Brothers?" Extensions of this line of thought would lead to many new basic discoveries.

There is one big, deep, serious trap into which those who are interested in exploring this type of research may fall. Mere spending of money for basic financial research will not bring significant results. It would seem logical that those who are skilled in finance could do this type of work and that a person with a great reputation in finance would produce the desired results. The trap is that one must wipe clean his slate of knowledge about present thought patterns and deliberately create new thought patterns and viewpoints. Those who have skill in finance will be helpful in evaluating the work, but the probability is small that they can create the new thought patterns and viewpoints. Legions of examples have proved this.

Another trap which must be avoided is the assumption that mathematics is the prime requisite for the basic researcher. Very little has been created through the use of mathematics; mathematical science is superb only as an analytical tool after new thought patterns and goals have been created. In past years many have considered mathematics and basic research almost inseparable, but this is a fundamental error.

Another mistake is to get a man of national reputation justly earned in politics, industry, or academic life and make him responsible for the project. He will not know how to select men or how to lead the organization.

Basic Research in the Financial World

Howard C. Tharsing
Partner
Dean Witter & Company

AREAS for basic research, as basic research is defined by the symposium committee, appear so numerous that a basic research project might well be set up to determine just what should be researched. Among the more important in my view are:

1. Relationship of the financial world with owners of business enterprises (i.e., stockholders).

2. The financial community's code of ethics.

3. Role of the financial community in providing guidance to management in such fields as –

    a. Conflict of interest.

    b. Relationships with public institutions.

    c. Relationships with owners.

4. The trend or direction in which financial institutions are moving and the tools available either to accelerate the trend or to change the direction.

5. What are the problems of communication most directly concerning the financial community? What are the tools or methods available to improve the financial community's contact with other segments of the economy?

In regard to the relationship of the financial community with owners it would appear that one project could explore the historical relationship when capital was scarce, the changes in the relationship – in part under the influence of the public sector (?) or by default (?) – and the possible relationships which can be developed in order that owners may most effectively contribute to the future progress of our society.

The question of the relationship of the financial community with business owners seems to me to be worth considerable research effort. On one hand, we are attempting materially to expand the ownership of business by all classes of society. On the other hand, we appear to have no, or little, understanding of how these new owners can best be advised as to both the obligations and the privileges of ownership. Perhaps the basic subject for research here is: Are financial institutions chiefly a conduit for funds – with very limited responsibilities – or should they act as "trustees" for the principals in that they should provide the owner with facts and recommendations for action? This question obviously ties in with the opportunity to regain the initiative relative to the public sector. This project might overlap or be a part of a more complete study of the ethical code of the financial community or of a project looking toward an examination of the basic factors of owner responsibility – rather than a project directly concerned with the financial community.

A research project considering the ethical code of the financial community should not develop a code of practice in my opinion and probably could not do so anyway. Rather it would review the development of the present code and the history of change; it would consider what trends are evident and the reasons therefor. I believe this is a most important area for investigation and study since it could provide the basis for a broader understanding of cause and effect and, hopefully, a foundation for future action. This seems to me to be important if the financial community is to develop a position which will be considerably less vulnerable to attack from the public sector. The right project in this area might enable the financial community to assume leadership in a field of increasing public concern. The need for strong leadership and the prestige of such leadership are of considerable magnitude in my opinion. If this appraisal is correct, leadership in this area could be useful in checking the expansion of the public sector. Moreover, development of a sound foundation of "professional practice" might be of considerable help in strengthening the confidence of the financial community in itself and its future. It could also improve the usefulness of the community to society as a whole (in addition to its economic usefulness) and possibly could reduce the fairly high degree of provincialism which often seems to pervade the Street. I do not mean to imply that this research should be applied research despite these hopes.

A research project to examine the relationships between the financial community and management is of major importance because we no longer have the leverage which was once provided by a scarcity of capital, which was often useful in getting management attention. With more funds and a higher percentage of capital requirements being generated internally, professional managers have less urgent reasons for direct contact with the financial community. This is a very broad field and could possibly be subdivided into a number of projects such as (a) areas for financial community and management cooperation in developing owner communication channels, (b) the role of the financial community in aiding management to develop public relations including government relations, (c) the question of conflict of interest and the community's role in aiding management. It is obviously important for the financial community to be able to work with managers in providing *constructive* leadership in the private sector of the economy *if* the private sector is to regain the initiative. This also seems to be an area where the confidence of the general public can be gained by proper action on the part of the financial community. One subproject might be concerned with the role of the financial community in assisting management to provide information for the proper valuation of securities. Obviously fluctuations in security prices resulting from lack of proper information can damage the position of both management and the financial community. The experience in this area following the 1929 crash and a number of subsequent reactions including that of Texas Gulf Sulphur seem to provide ample evidence that regardless of our best efforts our communications or methods are not providing the best results.

This in turn suggests that another area for study could well include the subject of cooperation between the financial community and management in improvement and agreement on accounting concepts. This whole area of management relationships may be a most useful one in which to enlist the cooperation of educational institutions because of their great facility for communication with the present generation of professional management.

With respect to the trend or direction in which financial institutions are moving, it is probably self-evident that basic research in this field is needed to define the areas which concern us and to diagnose the causes of our concern. This is prerequisite to a solution or solutions to our problems. In this regard I believe it would be useful to consider the levers available to the community in the past with which it could influence the direction of the economy, the levers now available – used or unused – and the levers which may become available in the future.

Perhaps the most significant area for research is, as in many other segments of the economy, the area of communication. Inability to convey ideas clearly, particularly in a community dealing largely in intangibles, is obviously a problem of considerable importance. (Consider, for example, the language of the prospectus). Such a research project presumably would investigate not only the historical development of the financial "idiom" but also the channels for the dissemination of ideas. This could include consideration of means of communication with owners, with management, with government, with educators, and with the public generally. The possibility of disseminating ideas to as well as through educational institutions and consideration of opportunities and methods for exchange of ideas with secondary school and university faculties might well be part of such a project.

It is in the foregoing areas that real opportunities for basic research seem to me to be present.

The Implications for Management of Today's "Guesstimates" about Tomorrow

Charles B. Harding
Retired Chairman of the Board
Smith, Barney & Co., Incorporated

THE investment banking business has never been noted for its management techniques, probably because it is a kind of "professional business" and most of the people in it are engaged in a specialty of their own. Very few of them develop into managers or generals. It is, nevertheless, important that good management, whatever the business, look to the future, think about the future, and plan to guide its organization so as to take maximum advantage of new developments. Tomorrow does come.

Some years ago I heard "Boss" Kettering, a former vice president in charge of research and development for General Motors, talk about inventions. He said he was not a scientist and held no degrees. He was a tinkerer, but the one thing he had learned in his life of tinkering, which produced such inventions as the self-starter, was that everybody looks first for the solution to the problem. Kettering said, "You never solve a problem by looking for the solution. The first thing you have to do is to find out what the problem is, and once you've defined the problem in proper terms, the solutions will come by themselves."

Before one can consider the "implications for management of today's 'guesstimates' about tomorrow," it is necessary to look at both the total trends of society and the specific trends of a given business. This will give the scope of the problem. For example, looking parochially at some of the specifics of the investment banking business, I realize that we should have

started thinking some years ago about such suggestive trends
as:

1. The increase in the number of private businesses that are
going public.

2. The amount of corporate financing that is coming from
internal sources.

3. The growing New York Stock Exchange volume.

4. The growth in the number of stockholders.

5. The growing amounts of common stock held by such institutions as pension funds, mutual funds, and insurance companies.

6. The narrowing spreads in corporate underwritings.

7. The growing demand for municipal money.

8. The increase in corporate financing by private placement.

Additionally, we must always be considering such things as
population growth, international developments, and the increase
in the GNP.

Each manager must ask what impact the pertinent trends will
have for his own business and what he can do about it. It
seems to me there are three possibilities. One solution is to do
the best you can to work out a plan for your own future. Of
course, since the New Deal days "planning" has been a dirty
word, but that is because all too often it refers to the kind of
planning that the government does, which results, in the
end, in controlling the economy. A second course is to continue
taking on more people without regard to what you are going to
do with them, adding people to your organization on the assumption that you are going to be bigger and therefore are going
to need more people. The third possibility is to do nothing at
all–to go on as you are now and hope that something will hap-
pen to take care of you. To me, the latter course is the surest
way to go out of business. No business is the same from one
year to the next. New factors are constantly coming into it, and
only those organizations that are able to adapt themselves
to changing conditions are able to survive.

If your decision is that you want to plan, the question is how
to go about it. In my opinion, the first thing you have to do is
decide on your firm's objective. Our firms are not all alike.

Practically speaking, probably no two firms are exactly alike. You have to decide what kind of firm you want to be, what kind of business you want to do. You should also be sure that that business is compatible with the people you have in your firm. It may be possible, if you decide that a different kind of business is very attractive, for you to change your people, but this takes time and is very difficult.

If you do not have your objectives clearly in mind, it is very hard to do any planning to meet them. If one of your objectives is to make money – and most of us have this as at least one of our objectives – a study of the costs and the profitability of the various activities you are engaged in would seem logical.

In the investment banking business, unfortunately, we are about fifty years behind other industries in developing reasonably valuable cost figures. It is difficult to decide, for instance, that the underwriting business is attractive and we ought to increase our efforts in it if we don't know how much money we are actually making in the underwriting business.

The obvious difficulty, of course, is that we lump certain expenses in one pot. We know what we gross from different activities, but we don't know how to allocate expenses. This is a side of our business that I think deserves a great deal of study and effort (by all of us, working with our accountants and other people). We should try to improve this tool – income and expense analysis by type of activity – to enable us not only to plan but to make corrections in the way we do business and to have some control over costs.

To begin to plan, the idea of planning must be accepted by at least the top people in your organization. It is not easy to get people to accept planning. It means a great change in the thinking of most executives. In the investment banking business, for example, executives tend to use a kind of trader's "opportunistic flexible reaction to stimuli" approach to business. You may encounter old gentlemen with hardening of the arteries who resist change of any kind. You may also run up against the argument that this kind of thing "does not apply to our business." We have all heard people say, whenever we discuss anything new, "Well, our business is different and this doesn't apply." In the investment banking business, older executives tend to favor "feel" rather than a factual approach because this places a premium on their greatest asset – experience.

Once you gain the acceptance of the idea of planning, however, you have these great advantages:

1. A plan gives direction to the firm's efforts.

2. It provides a standard for measuring the progress of both the firm and the individual.

3. It tends to draw the firm together in a team for a united purpose.

4. It saves you an immense amount of time in making policy decisions. Almost every day something comes up about which you have to decide: Should we do it or not? If you have a general plan, you can say, "Does this fit in with the plan or doesn't it?"

5. It improves morale and productivity because all the employees in your organization will understand that you know where you are going. This potential improvement in management effectiveness has perhaps the greatest implications of long-range planning for management.

The question now is: How do you go about it? Who does the planning? Again, there are three possible ways that I see to do it.

1. The executives of the firm can do it themselves, a course which has certain advantages. They know their business; they know the subject. It is their plan, and therefore they are more likely to carry it out than if it came to them from others. It provides them with a certain amount of education about their own business, and they can make the necessary decisions to go ahead with the plan.

The disadvantage of having planning done by management is that management people tend to have preconceived ideas. You may have personality conflicts in your organization. Most of us have not had experience in planning, and there may be certain departments which exhibit too much self-interest in defending their own way of doing things. If a change is suggested, they may consider it an indictment of present management.

2. Outside consultants may be employed. The advantage of

doing this is that outsiders are unbiased. They have had experience in doing this kind of work, often have devoted all their time to it. They can be faster and they can bring to you the experience of other organizations for which they have worked.

The disadvantage of this method is that it costs more. Also, consultants tend to have a generalized approach and may lack knowledge about your business.

3. Another way – and this is the way we chose in my own company – is to use members of your own staff, preferably the younger ones. The advantage here is that they know the business. Also, the cost is much less than employing outside people. There will probably be fewer personality conflicts, too, than there would be if either top management people or suspect outsiders took on the job.

The disadvantage is that staff members may lack experience in planning. They may also be in a weak bargaining position from which to get their ideas across to the bosses, and they don't make the final decisions. But, for better or for worse, that is the way we have tried it on this go-around.

The method of our group was to talk with as many people as possible in and out of the firm. This wide consultation developed many new ideas and made our own people feel that they were part of the overall project. The emphasis on internal participation through the planning group was very productive. Most management engineers put in their recommendations ideas they obtained from your own organization. You can do this same kind of job with your own staff. Moreover, it is remarkable how much information is available from trade sources like the New York Stock Exchange and from competitors. We find that a great many of our competitors are interested in this subject and are very glad to exchange information with us. Many of the top and middle management people in an organization have good ideas which have been burning in their heads for years, just waiting for somebody to come and ask for them.

The planner's job is to collate, analyze, and integrate all of these ideas, and then to write them down. He must be free from organizational pressure. The use of charts and graphs is very helpful. And it is most important that the planning report be written in English that can be readily understood.

An important step is to be sure that all the people who are involved in making decisions really understand, that they see the trends, the dangers, and the potentials. Merely giving them a document to read is not necessarily the answer. You may have to sit down with them and discuss it and even argue about it.

It is important that the top people want to have a plan, either because they want to make more money in the business or because they want long-range betterment of the firm – to have pride in the firm and in its future. They must believe in some desirable goal that will motivate them to accept planning and make it work.

At this point I shall give you a few quotations which may help in selling planning to your organization. Planning is something of a nuisance. Everyone would like to go about his daily business. To have to take time off to sweat over and study planning is not altogether appealing. As a prime sales document, we may start out with a quotation from Lincoln: "If we could first know where we are and whither we are tending, we could better judge what to do and how to do it."

Taylor, the father of scientific management tells us: "The use of long-range planning techniques is what distinguishes twentieth century from nineteenth century management."

In the *Harvard Business Review* of March, 1957, Payne says: "Long-range planning is the one really new technique left to management that gives a company a major competitive advantage."

Ewing's book, *Long Range Planning for Management,* states: "A well-communicated, well-understood program for the next five years should counteract cynicism about how top management decisions are made. It will give supervisors down the line the feeling that we know where we are going and not just that we are going somewhere."

I have tried to point out to my colleagues that we are all in the position of examining other companies to see how they do things, and we would consider any company to be poorly managed that did not have a plan and make a careful appraisal of its prospects and operating methods. We ourselves should do what we expect other people to do.

Once you have the plan and it has been approved by top management, the problem is to inform everybody in the organization about it and then try to get them behind it; otherwise it does no good to have a plan. This is a matter of communication, which is always a problem.

Everyone must know that the top person in the organization is in favor of the plan and has approved it. He is perhaps the only one who has the over-all viewpoint of the organization and the time to get away from the day-to-day routine. He is the only one with disciplinary power over vice presidents and partners, whichever they are, to put steam behind the plan and have it *carried out*. However, communicating with your organization means, first, seeing that your top people, and through them their staffs, want to participate so that the planning comes from them rather than being delivered to them as a ukase from on high.

No plan is going to be carried out exactly the way it is written. That is obvious. You should not present it as something that is rigid and inflexible and give the impression that "this is the way it's going to be." But it does serve as a guidepost and when you vary from it, you know that you are varying and you know the reasons.

Particularly in the early stages, definite requirements of scope and timing for the people that are doing the planning must be set and adhered to. If you give the planning project to people in your organization who have other work to do and you say, "Well, do this when you can," it may take five years to get it done. You should give them a deadline by which they must deliver it to you. If you don't do that, you may never get it.

It should also be made clear to the group that is working on the project that the time and effort spent in these endeavors are just as important as their regular jobs and that at the end of the operation they will be rewarded. What the reward will be, of course, is up to the individual firm.

In a study of this kind, the question always comes up as to whether you should try to improve your own operation as you are now doing it or branch out into various other forms of service. I hope that many of you have read the article "Marketing Myopia" by Levitt in the July 1960 *Harvard Business Review.* It is one of the best articles they have ever published.

He emphasizes that the important thing is to find out what your customers want that you are not giving them and then to figure out what they are going to want in the next five years so that you can prepare your organization to deliver new services if they are not now available in your firm.

The great thing about Ford was not that he initiated the five-dollar-a-day minimum wage or that he was a production genius. The really great contribution that he made to the industry was his finding out that people would buy a good car for $500. Ford went further. He was able to get the price down to $295. Having found out what his customers wanted, he took the necessary steps to produce a car for a price that they liked, which he did, and it went like hot cakes – 15 million by 1927. These were the rewards of giving customers what they wanted. Ford's policy in the years immediately after 1927 demonstrated what happens when you don't meet customers' wants. Thus, in one organization, we have a wonderful illustration of this basic principle – when it was followed and when it was not.

If you can find out what services your customers want – and one good way to find out is to ask them – and then deliver those services, you will find that you are in a very good competitive position. But you must not repeat Ford's mistake and think customers' wants never change. You must be alert and anticipate change.

Plans which involve new areas, new people, new requirements, and new problems should be approached cautiously. Diversification holds at least as much risk as promise. I am talking about getting into a completely different kind of business, such as real estate financing or leasing or various other things that many of us do not now do. They can all look terribly attractive when you first study them, but you may not realize the amount of time and effort it takes to do them. Not having been in them, you may not realize that you lack the skills to do them. Most careful studies will show tremendous potentials in improving existing endeavors without the need of risking further diversification. Did you ever consider how many customers for your present business you do not now have – that someone else has?

Almost every study will show the need for improved internal financial control to give the data on which to base decisions. I mentioned this before and I would like to mention it again because it is so very important.

Now that you have the plan and have communicated it to everybody, how do you go about making the decisions as to which parts of it you want to implement and how you are going to do it? I believe that one way to do it would be to sit down with the partner in charge and the key man in each department of your organization and discuss the part of the plan that applies to their department, so that each department comes back to the partnership or to the management with its segment of the plan which they have studied and argued about and finally approved. Then synthesize all the plans rather than have a town meeting in the beginning where all the department heads argue about one another's departments. This is merely a theory on my part because we haven't tried it yet. However, don't overlook the ideas of Chairman of the Board Givens of American Brake Shoe in his book, *Reaching Out in Management.* His thesis is that all departments can contribute ideas to the management of others. In American Brake Shoe he found that some of the best ideas for production came from people in purchasing, and so on. He frequently rotated his people through departments that were not in their fields of specialization.

The implications of any plan that you work out will finally be interpreted in terms of people. To me, this is the greatest value of the plan because you will know what kinds of people you want to hire and what kinds of training you want to give them in order to be sure that you will have the numbers you need at the time you need them. My firm spends a great deal of time trying to develop a good training program, and I think the first and most important part of it is the selection of the people we want to train. In doing this, we try to look for three things; first, aptitude for the business; second, motivation to go into the business and to succeed; and, third, good character.

Determining aptitudes is relatively simple, but determinating motivation is difficult because motivations change. I think it is most important, however, to stress good character. The guts of it is getting the right people into an organization at the bottom and then seeing that they don't stay there! All of the best plans in the world will not produce success without the right people. In all of your planning you must start and end with people.

PART II

Appraising the Changing Structure, Functions, and Services of the Financial World

Commentary

FOUR thoughtful memoranda, written independently of each other, are here grouped under a single heading which, however infelicitous its phrasing, may serve to indicate their common elements. While these papers naturally differ in detail, they have essentially the same focus. It seems of some significance that among the contributions to this symposium there were in fact four discussions characterized by this same concern.

All these papers stress the great and rapid changes currently taking place throughout the financial world – in its structure and practices, in the roles of different types of institutions, in the size and types of funds flowing through these bodies, in governmental regulations. Reading between the lines of these discussions a possible conclusion may be reached: If we ever had an adequate definition of the capital markets and the financial world, that definition is almost certainly inadequate for the new and rapidly evolving situation with which we are now confronted. From this tentative hypothesis a number of tantalizing questions can be derived, important both for the economy as a whole and for particular financial institutions.

If we cannot define the capital markets with any precision, are we in a position to appraise them?

Are the types of statistics and the analytical constructs developed during the past generation adequate for the present situation? That is, do the data that we are accustomed to use, when analyzed by familiar processes, give answers that are comparable to the answers so developed ten, twenty, and thirty years ago, let alone answers adequate for our present needs?

Real skepticism is permissible. It is not certain that the data still mean what they once did. While many examples could be advanced, a striking case in point is the great change during recent years in the structure of both the assets and liabilities of the commercial banking system.

A third question perhaps can be phrased as follows: Even if we were sure that particular portions of the framework of governmental regulations that guide financial institutions – a framework that has been worked out since, say, the passage of the Federal Reserve Act – were adequate and proper in their contemporary situations, can we have equal confidence in their propriety in the light of the developing circumstances spelled out so admirably in Ora C. Roehl's paper? Again some skepticism seems reasonable. A good example of what is referred to here, not original with this symposium, is the apparently diminishing area in which monetary policy can quickly be made effective.

Finally, if we have some difficulty in defining capital markets and understanding their processes, do we have a firm basis for assessing whether their operations help or hinder attainment of national objectives? Answers to this question cannot be given without considering the needs of the Treasury and the management of the federal debt, in connection with the needs of the private sector of the economy. And while monetary theory and fiscal policy furnish some of the material needed for an answer, it seems clear that these constructs do not – at least, as commonly defined – supply all of the framework necessary as a basis for judgment.

The Role and Functions of Financial Institutions: A Few General and Random Notes on Needed Basic Research

Ora C. Roehl
Financial and
Management Consultant

THERE is concern these days about the lack of basic research in the financial world. These general notes have been prepared in an effort to outline some of the basic research areas that should be explored "with reference to the services and functions the financial world might or should perform for the public generally and the whole economy, particularly the private sector" and also to indicate "what the behavior and characteristics of financial institutions and the private financial world should be if they are to act as an effective check on the expansion of the public sector."

Basic research for the purpose of these notes is defined as "research and speculative thinking undertaken not with reference to immediate profit, present practice or the existing structure of the financial world."

FINANCIAL INSTITUTIONS – THE FINANCIAL WORLD

Financial Institutions – What Are They?

The Report of the President's Committee on Financial Institutions (the so-called Heller Report) considers financial institutions to be mainly "private institutions that accept deposits and shares" – national banks, federal savings and loan organizations, and federal credit unions.

The Department of Commerce among its industry classifications has one that includes banking; credit agencies other than banks; security and commodity brokers, dealers, exchanges, and services; insurance carriers; insurance agents, brokers, and services; real estate; combinations of real estate, insurance, loan, and law offices; and holding and other investment companies – all in a single industry group.

Generally, when one talks about financial institutions, banks, insurance companies, finance companies, and investment companies immediately come to mind. But as one thinks a moment about the list one finds that the list needs to be divided into many subdivisions.

In the field of banking there are large commercial banks with associated trust companies, small commercial banks, country banks, mutual savings banks, and federal savings and loan companies. Even companies such as Commercial Credit are calling themselves banks.

In the insurance field there are mutual life insurance companies, stock life companies, fire and casualty companies, health and accident insurance companies, other more specialized insurance companies, and many and varied kinds of combination companies.

In the credit company field there are personal loan companies, automobile financing companies, factoring companies, leasing companies, and credit insurance companies.

Included in the investment companies are the open-end funds (some with and some without sales charges), closed-end investment companies, many types of specialized investment companies, and various types of mutual fund sales organizations.

Even these subdivisions do not complete the list of financial institutions. Other business activities must be included such as noninsured pension funds both private and public, the trust departments of banks as well as certain specialized trust companies, mortgage bankers, real estate trusts, leasing companies, the stock exchange members, investment bankers, over-the-counter dealers, and the firms making up the so-called third market.

Perhaps for the purpose of this review the National Association of Security Dealers as well as the New York and regional exchanges should be considered as being financial institutions.

And what about college endowment and charitable foundations? They also exhibit many of the characteristics of financial institutions.

The Financial World: Its Services and Functions

In order to determine, even in a once-over-lightly sort of way, areas where fundamental research is needed in the financial world, one needs to look at the business these financial institutions are in and the services they now render or could render to the general public in the future.

As these services are listed, one finds very few services performed by the financial institutions that are not highly competitive. About the only area almost entirely reserved for a single institution is bank checking and deposit accounts, but here too the competition between banks in many areas of the country is extremely fierce.

A random list of the competitive services rendered by the financial institutions includes:

Deposit and check-cashing services
Management services
Computer services
Automobile and other durable goods financing
Selection of investments
Custodianship of securities
Management of securities
Management of property
Collection of dividends and interest
Provision of meeting places, steamship, airplane, and theatre tickets
Annuities and pensions
Variable annuities
Life insurance
Realty insurance
Accident insurance

Term insurance of all types
Personal loans
Home improvement loans
Financial planning
Home mortgages
Family budgeting
Accumulation and withdrawal plans
Safe deposit boxes
Mortgage insurance
Mortgage servicing
Equipment leasing
Stock and bond sales and purchases
Life insurance companies' special and segregated accounts
Factoring services
Credit cards
Revolving credit plans

Credit insurance	Title insurance
Real estate and special	Investment counseling
building financing	Auto and travel clubs
Educational financing plans	Rental cars
Travel loans	

The Great Transformation

Great changes are taking place in the financial business. The transformation that financial institutions and the financial world are going through both structurally and functionally is similar to that affecting business generally. Everybody is getting into everybody else's business. The commercial banks are trying to stop the mutual savings banks from invading the regular banking business. The bank trust departments and mutual savings banks are expanding into the investment company business. For example, National City Bank of New York and National Bank of Detroit have registered their plans with the SEC. The New York Stock Exchange has its Monthly Investment Plan. Investment houses own mutual funds. Investment bankers have long found that the competition with direct bond placements is reducing their regular investment banking business, and today direct placement of equity securities is becoming more and more common.

Not only are the financial institutions getting more and more into each other's business, but other businesses are finding that the financial business looks like a mighty green pasture. Merchandising companies such as Sears Roebuck, J. C. Penney, and Carson Pirie Scott are entering the insurance, mutual fund, finance company, and banking fields. Thalheimer Brothers has set up an insurance agency, but I. Magnin backed away from a similar plan after its customers objected.

Hamilton Management has been bought by ITT; Citizens and Southern National Bank, Georgia's largest, is preparing to go into the insurance business with its people acting as agents for insurance companies. Such action threatens to blow up into a nationwide battle between the insurance companies and their present agencies. A savings and loan company in Denver is now owned by MCA. Avco has purchased Delta Finance. Swift has long found Globe Insurance a significant contributor to its profits.

Citizens and Southern and National City Bank of New York are in the factoring business. Eaton & Howard is setting up a trust company. Fireman's Fund and other insurance companies are establishing holding companies to own various kinds of financial institutions including mutual funds. Boston Safe Deposit and Trust has done likewise and has set up a holding company – the Boston Company – to enable it to expand more readily into other fields.

"Account selling," whereby insurance agents furnish their clients insurance, mutual funds, title insurance, and all sorts of financial and related services, is growing within the insurance business.

Dow Chemical has established a bank for investment finance in Zurich. Transamerica is called a "department store of finance." Standard Oil, Socony Mobil, and Texaco are selling insurance and other services and even merchandise such as radios to their nationwide group of credit card holders. Chrysler and Volkswagen have set up insurance companies. Fidelity Fund's Crosby Corporation and Continental Assurance have developed a plan for the joint sale of Fidelity Capital Fund and Continental ordinary life and disability insurance.

The whole field has attracted so much general attention that a new mutual fund – Pilgrim Financial and Growth Fund – has even been established to invest only in companies in the "money business," e.g., insurance, banks, and finance companies.

Institutions continue to grow. For example, a study at the University of Michigan has concluded that stock ownership by individuals will decline in the decade from 1965 to 1975 from $286 billion to $269 billion, whereas holdings of financial intermediaries will increase from $144 billion to $254 billion. In the past decade the stock holdings of individuals have increased less than 20 percent, whereas institutional holdings have increased almost 75 percent. Thus the institutionalization of the nation's securities markets continues – with the over-all impact on the nation's business still clouded.

A transformation is going on in the financial professional

field. An organization of chartered financial analysts has been established, which should result in a substantial improvement in the quality of the work and standards of financial analysts. This organization is still in its infancy, but the members undoubtedly have research studies under consideration that will make a contribution to the financial institutions they serve. Certified public accountants have long served the needs of business, and in recent years they have become more active in the financial world. Many of the accounting firms are expanding their services to include estate planning, personal financial planning, and management consulting, and the American Institute of Certified Public Accountants is actively sponsoring basic research as to other possible services.

GOVERNMENTAL FINANCIAL INSTITUTIONS

The Public Sector – Also "Great Expansion"

While the importance of private financial institutions, both in assets under control and in services rendered, has grown much faster than the general economy, governmental financial institutions have also multiplied and grown.

The Home Loan Bank, the FHA, the SBA, the VA, the REA, the Department of Agriculture, and the Antipoverty Program have put and continue to put the government into the financial business in a major way. Not only does the government furnish funds to the banking industry and insure bank deposits, but it furnishes funds for everything from a rural electrical cooperative to a neighborhood beauty parlor.

The federal regulatory agencies such as the FRB, FDIC, Comptroller of the Currency, and the SEC have not been seeing eye to eye on regulatory policies and practices, and Congress is considering action. Government stabilization policies, the effectiveness of the nation's lending institutions, the solvency and liquidity of private financial institutions and the possible strengthening of competition among such institutions, reserve requirements, interest rate regulation, portfolio regulation, conflicts of interest, bank mergers, and the possibility of federal charters for life insurance companies are other "Washington" topics affecting the financial world and discussed in the daily papers.

In the fields of foreign trade, investment and banking, government agencies have set up voluntary programs whereby businesses and banking are to help reduce the United States balance of payments deficit.

All sorts of guidelines affecting the financial world are being established, and government control via guidelines is growing throughout the business world. One financial leader says, "The guideline approach represents a giant step away from self-reliance and personal responsibility, and toward federal domination of our national economy." Other businessmen talk about social responsibility and feel that as long as business can demonstrate that it is able to solve the problems which need to be solved, it will be left free to solve them.

Many of the government's activities in the financial field are said to have been designed to fill a void left by private financial institutions. It is even said that Medicare became a law in 1965 principally because the medical profession and the insurance companies were ten years too late in providing needed health and medical insurance. As a result, the government has expanded its activities into what was once a private enterprise area, and the insurance industry stands to lose what was becoming a profitable and important part of its business.

Pressures for some sort of over-all governmental and business planning are also building up – a controversial area to say the least.

Some weeks ago *Business Week* said that "some leading business executives are moving toward the conclusion that the dangers to their own freedom, and to society's, will be reduced rather than increased if a new balance – involving elements of both cooperation and conflict – can be worked out between business and government."

With the great transformation in the financial world and with the great importance of financial institutions to the nation's economy, it appears that there exist both plenty of room and a great need for many basic research programs –

programs that would not only help the financial world but also contribute to the general welfare.

BASIC RESEARCH AREAS

What are some of the basic research areas that should be explored?

In the scientific world basic or fundamental research has long been the foundation on which applied research is built. If the prime aim of a project is fuller knowledge of a phenomenon, the work is placed in the basic research category; the practical application of the new knowledge is applied research. The past twenty-five years have seen a great growth in scientific research, and while there are many complaints about the need for more basic research, yet the whole research effort is well supported by the government and industry to the tune of close to $20 billion a year, of which about 5 percent is spent on basic research.

In the financial world solid basic research is still very much in the developing stage. Research in the financial field is still too much concerned with the rationalization of the *status quo*, and a rationalization effort is not research. It is rather an effort to defend existing conditions, whether they are good or bad, and it is the antithesis of the search for truth. Many financial institutions have set up research departments, but they are generally oriented to market research, although some do get into technological developments concerned with computers and other means to facilitate mechanical operations.

Freedom of inquiry, which is essential in basic research, probably cannot exist in the average financial institution. Financial basic research is still in the stage of development where university-sponsored research activity or a center for advanced study is needed to undertake true basic research. But here again problems arise because many of the questions that need attention are so colored with political overtones that free inquiry and search for truth and facts are hampered.

In the scientific world much progress has been made in understanding how the scientist ascertains facts and obtains new knowledge, how he comprehends new relationships, and how research programs should be organized and conducted. But very little know-how has been developed in what might be called social studies research or political science research.

With these few general observations on research in mind, let us turn to research areas where any number of worth-while basic research projects can be uncovered.

I. The Status of Basic Research in the Financial World

A first project might well be set up to review financial research reports that have been prepared in the past to determine their general quality (have the reports clearly indicated what is cause and what are symptoms?) and objectivity. A general determination could be attempted to see whether the reports have added to fundamental knowledge and how they might be improved. This would require some definition of fundamental knowledge.

Research in the scientific area usually starts with a review of the literature; hence a program that contemplates basic research in the financial field might well start out with a review of what has been done and is being done and how much is truly basic research.

Can any conclusions be arrived at concerning the quality of work done by certain institutions and individuals? This would require some determination of how quality can be measured. Perhaps change is so prevalent in the financial world that the report writers need to be economic biochemists. As one writer says, life is not logical, it is biological. This may mean that basic research in the social sciences will be more difficult than it is in scientific areas where basic discoveries are less subject to change.

The NBER, the CED, the Twentieth Century Fund, the Research Branch of the AMA, and many other organizations are doing research work. A survey of their projects and reports should be helpful as such a review might show where the voids exist, not only in basic research but also in terms of organizations capable of doing the work. Very likely some new centers for basic research need to be established.

II. The Role of Government

A first project in this area might be to ascertain what government financial support, if any, should be given to research in the financial world. In the scientific field government grants support a major part of the nation's basic research effort, and the National Science Foundation and the Defense Department are very active. Some scientific researchers feel that government has assumed too great a role. The President has a scientific adviser and he also has the CEA, but the scientific adviser seems much more concerned with basic research than is the Council. A project could well be established to develop some ideas on what the government's participation in basic financial research should or should not be.

Other areas for basic exploration of the government's role might include the following:

1. What about planning? Planning is talked about a great deal these days; it's popular in France, the Netherlands, and most European countries. One foreign minister recently said about his country's plan: "The plan is conceived as an instrument by which public investment is to be disciplined, the economic policy of the various ministerial departments is to be coordinated and complete information may be offered on future developments of the national economy. Economic planning, thus understood, is nowadays accepted everywhere." This hardly seems like a good answer for the United States.

Why is planning so much talked about? What should the financial world do about it? Some good basic research projects could uncover a few answers.

2. What about taxation? Could tax incentives be used more extensively to encourage economic development in areas where private enterprise has not been too active – areas that are not the proper sphere for government activity? The SBIC's are an example of the type of companies fostered by tax incentives.

The whole area concerned with the taxation of financial institutions is just full of project ideas.

3. What about international finance? The internationalization of business continues at a great pace. Dow Chemical has recently established a bank in Zurich; Monsanto has developed a new convertible bond to be sold abroad which will eventually be convertible into the United States company's common stock.

Balance of payment problems have caused the government to restrict foreign investments and thus have restricted freedom of action in the financial world.

Good unbiased basic research projects on this whole subject covering the responsibilities of the United States companies and the role of the government would definitely be helpful.

4. What about credit controls? Today a significant amount of the nation's short-term financing is done outside the banking system. Many large corporations loan their excess funds in competition with the banks. Annual withdrawals of home real estate equities is now approaching annual debt amortizations, and monetization of property values is adding $14 billion to $15 billion a year to the spending stream.

Basic research might help to determine the government's responsibilities in this very difficult area. Research might also help to develop principles to guide the lending activities of both financial and nonfinancial institutions.

5. What changes are needed in government financial institutions? All is not happy today between the FRB, the Comptroller of the Currency, the SEC, the CEA, and other governmental financial institutions. Oftentimes their actions on mergers and regulations are at cross purposes. Basic research projects covering the duties and the functions of government financial institutions are needed.

There are, of course, many other governmental problems that can stand a bit of basic research in addition to those listed above. The major governmental problem is probably the nation's monetary system. This subject is so fundamental, and so important to the financial world, that it could well be the basis for any number of studies. It is an area where financial institutions might well do some serious thinking about what they should do to keep the dollar sound.

III. The Institutionalization of Securities Markets

Considerable concern is being expressed about what is called the "paraproprietal society." It is said that investment companies are now socializing the wealth of that great domain of capitalism, the corporation. Drucker has called today's fiduciary managers the new tycoons. He points out that "the democratization of business ownership by the fiduciary investor is an achievement without parallel in economic or social history, but it is also a perplexing one."

A New York Stock Exchange report says that by 1970 financial institutions will own over 30 per cent of the stocks listed on the Exchange, and that the 1970 market will be vastly different from today's. One financial writer declares that if the process continues after 1970, with institutions buying and not selling, the market will not merely be vastly different; it may not even exist.

A recent book, *The Silent Partners: Institutional Investors and Corporate Control*, by Baum and Stiles, raises many provocative questions about the great transformation that is going on today through the institutionalization of the securities markets. In his introduction to the book Harbrecht says:

> The problem of economic power that results from the large size of modern enterprise, the structure of industry, the influence of our financial institutions are all matters of public policy, going to the question of what kind of society we want to live in. As things stand there is no clear goal or national criterion which we can use to determine whether modern changes are leading us where we want to go.

He goes on to say that the trend in the institutionalization of investments

> provides us with a good object lesson in the process of natural accretion by which a society shapes itself. Business and industry begin to take a certain course: that course is curbed and regulated but not stopped or reversed. Governmental agencies are established for the protection and assertion of the public interest and the courts in turn curb and regulate the action of the agencies. The result is that the steady thrust of the organizational advance of business and industry is, like a mighty river, channeled, directed, sometimes

diverted and somethimes accelerated, but never stopped. It is flowing onward, but where? . . .

New elements are constantly being introduced which force our economy to modify itself. Technology, for example, presents opportunities which can be exploited only by sophisticated organizations of wealth, managerial expertise, and highly trained scientists and technicians.

With these changes generated by technology in methods of production, transportation, and communication come profound changes in the scale of economic enterprise. The result is organization of human effort on a scale undreamed of even fifty years ago.

The whole subject is worthy of a great deal of basic research. It is an area where financial institutions might well determine what should and what should not be done. Only in this way can unsound regulation and deadening government interference be avoided.

IV. *Financial Institutions – Policies and Principles*

As mentioned earlier, everybody wants to get into the financial business these days. The reasons are not hard to find, for it is really about as good a growth industry as there is. The mutual funds' investments totaled about $11 billion in 1956 and will soon exceed $30 billion. Savings and loan assets have skyrocketed; pension fund assets of industry will grow from the present $77 billion to $225 billion by 1980, and state and municipal funds from $30 billion to $85 billion in the same period.

In the past decade short-term debt has increased twelve times, whereas disposable income has only tripled. In the last twenty years consumer credit has grown from $6 billion to $76 billion. Consumer credit, it is estimated, will grow 50 percent and installment credit 66 percent by 1970, with the ratio of debt to disposable income increasing from 14 percent to 16 percent.

The number of mutual funds has quadrupled since the war. The number of life insurance companies has grown from fewer than 400 twenty years ago to over 1,500 now, and in the interim 600 to 700 companies have merged. New savings and loan companies have blossomed throughout the country. From 1947 to 1960, 260 new national banks and 1,019 new state banks were established. Since 1961 another 460 national banks and 478 state banks have been organized.

In view of this great growth record and the potentials for profit it is not surprising that the financial world is going through a great transformation and that everybody wants to get into the business. The unfortunate thing is that some of the expansion and some of the new activities are unsound.

Some really thorough basic research not only would be a great help to financial institutions but also could contribute significant answers to some of the questions raised in Research Area III on the problems connected with the institutionalization of the securities markets and the concentration of corporate ownership. Among the many worth-while research projects that could be undertaken might be the following:

1. *What businesses are the financial companies in?* It would be interesting to know how many financial institutions have a written statement of their business policies and objectives and to know what such policy statements include. Such a basic research project would not only be helpful to existing financial institutions but would also be a guideline to companies contemplating entry into the financial world, many of whom do not appear to have a very good understanding of what it means to get into or be in the financial business. It might also be useful in drafting new regulatory and other legislation that may be deemed needed in the years ahead.

2. *What will be the impact of the great transformation in the financial world on specific financial institutions?* Investment banking houses and stock exchange members are now quite concerned about the problems that lie ahead, especially the impact of competitive factors and the threat of antitrust suits. Every financial institution is also concerned about the impact that the changing times will have on its business and what can be done about it. A thorough review of the changing trends in the financial world and their impact on various kinds of institutions would be worth while. Such a study would be of great help to institutions planning basic research to meet specific needs.

3. What about ethics and principles? In no business is there a greater need for a high degree of ethical conduct than in financial institutions. Certain companies have established principles to guide them. An examination in depth of such principles and a review of what might be considered ethical practices versus practices to be condemned might well be a subject for basic research. The results of such an examination might be used in setting regulatory guidelines.

4. What about the new economics? A good basic research project might concern itself with a review of the always emerging "new eras." How much of what makes up the new eras is based on fundamental change? How much only looks like basic change?

Some feeling exists today that the financial superstructure of the economy has grown faster than the underlying value stream. There has been a great tendency to stress growth in capital values.

U. S. News and World Report said some weeks ago that "many banks have changed their views on big government and big spending and have embraced the 'new economics' " of more government in business and ever more reliance on fiscal factors to stimulate the economy.

Perhaps a dispassionate review of bank economic publications – subjects discussed and conclusions arrived at over the years – might furnish data to show what if any real leadership the banks have been or are furnishing in the development of sound economic thinking and business principles. For example, what has been and is being said about the cost of consumer credit? Could the cost be reduced by innovations in the system? Would such reductions allow both more credit expansion and expansion on a healthier basis than we have at present?

Writing for "The Chase Economic Bulletin" issued by the Chase Bank in February 1929 Anderson compared the new era of 1921–28 with that of 1896–1903 and concluded that "it would be a mistake to try to draw any conclusions . . . with respect to timing of future events from the parallels between the two new eras." History repeats "but with great variations in the amount of time required for particular phases to recur."

Dr. Anderson also pointed out that it is safe to conclude that all "new eras" are not after all so very new in principle. Like causes produce like results – excessive gold and excessive bank reserves generate bank expansion, excessive bank expansion overflows into capital and speculative employments, and low interest rates and abundant credit will reflect themselves in rapidly rising capital values. The present era (1928) has been to a much greater extent financial than industrial or commercial; and it is felt that wealth is not being made by prosaic powers of work and saving out of income – rather wealth is to be made by rising capital values, and business is to be kept active by spending of profits made through rising capital values.

Dr. Anderson points out that in early 1929 investors believed that "stocks could not fall because the investment trusts would not let them." Present holders would not sell them "in view of the large taxes they would have to pay the government. Stocks were to be preferred ... because the bondholder only got his principal back ... whereas a stockholder could count on a steadily growing income ... and good opportunities not yet to be disclosed."

Anderson continues, "To the veteran who lived through the period of 1896–1903 this all has a very familiar sound ... that collective hypnotism ... finally captures even powerful intellects and able leaders."

This was said in early 1929, and perhaps there are no lessons to be learned from previous eras in 1966. Is any basic research, not research to justify various political points of view, possible that would bring light where we are still too much in the dark and where decisions have to be taken with only a limited perception of the relevant factors?

What about today's economy? Are institutions bidding up an ever-declining supply of stocks and putting too much money into the stock market – money which is not actually being put to productive use in the economy?

Are innovations needed in new money market instruments, such as new types of securities tied into tax advantages to funnel more private funds rather than government funds into needed expansion areas such as schools, power projects, and water systems?

Surely the lessons learned from the handling of the nation's money problems in the past must be there to help guide the present. Can more of them be uncovered and agreed to by good unbiased basic research? Surely this should be possible, and it would be worth a major effort. It must be remembered, however, that although a study of the past can discover certain fundamentals, progress demands innovations, new ways of doing things; and finding these new ways is really what basic research is supposed to do.

5. *What about the security markets?* The New York Stock Exchange, the American Exchange, and the regional exchanges are going through a transition period. Mutual funds are becoming members in the expectation of doing some of their own trading. The third market is furnishing buying and selling opportunities oftentimes at substantially reduced costs. The NASD is hard put to keep the over-the-counter market sound and liquid. There is room for some basic research studies in the whole important area of security trading and security markets.

V. The Needs of the Public

The man who foots the bills, the people who use and need the services of the financial institutions, the voters, the shareholders–all have a great stake in the progress of the financial world.

While change is a basic political and social fact, all change is not progress. Economic progress is essentially a continuing struggle between the call of the future and the defense of the *status quo.* Generally the longer the *status quo* holds out, the harder it is to get innovations accepted.

It is axiomatic that the centers of progress are also centers of disturbance. A progressive business is a dynamic one, and if financial institutions are not possessed of a certain amount of dynamics too, they will not grow but, as is the nature of all things, will deteriorate.

Acceleration is evident everywhere these days. Social changes around the world are being attempted in a period of twenty-five years that used to take a century. Whatever the reason, the pace is quickening in all business and governmental activities. Creativity and innovation are the bywords of today, and the future of individual financial companies will depend on how far ahead of this fast pace they can run.

Basic research into the needs of the public and into the needs of the customers of financial institutions would appear to offer many opportunities for analysis by companies and by other interested centers of research. Here are a few possible research projects.

1. What are the needs of the public? The basic needs served by financial institutions, such as insurance, savings, and credit, might well be thoroughly analyzed and the voids might be listed as they appear today – for example, better health insurance and lower cost of credit.

Speculative thinking about future needs should also be undertaken. In this way needs and problems may be identified and steps taken by financial institutions before the government or other institutions act on them.

2. What specific innovations would help the customer of today's financial institutions? A study of the trend of innovations in the financial world in the recent past and present, and guesses as to the future, could furnish ideas for a number of basic research projects.

The trend toward what is called "the all-finance route," whereby single companies try to furnish all the financial needs of a customer, is one area that can be explored to advantage. What are the good and bad points of this? Is it good for a bank to serve all a customer's insurance and investing needs? Is it good for a merchandising company to serve these needs? What types of know-how are necessary to serve the public best?

Another area for exploration might be the specific services themselves. Relatively new services include variable annuities, the Monthly Investment Plan of the New York Stock Exchange, mutual fund accumulation and withdrawal plans, insurance company separate accounts, and new combination fire and casualty insurance policies.

3. What about the shareholders? In the great transformation that is going on the shareholders of financial institutions sometimes seem to be neglected. There really should be some way to measure management performance. Observers are saying today that some sort of "economic performance accounting" should be developed. This would cover management compensation, the use made of corporate funds, the reinvestment of profits and returns received from such reinvestment, relative growth and profit analyses, competitive capabilities, and other factors which measure relative management performance. During a time of ever-increasing competition such a system of performance accounting might help management to meet its problems better. It appears to be an area worthy of a basic research project.

IN SUMMARY

Much has been said about the great growth in scientific knowledge, which is supposed to be doubling every nine years. Technological effort is doubling about every ten years; more advances have been made in science in the past fifty years than in all preceding history; and 90 per cent of the scientists who ever lived are probably still alive. It is also estimated that the United States will add as much to the GNP in the next ten years as was added in the entire two hundred years from colonial days to the 1950's – and that by 1975 the GNP will be double what it was in 1950.

The great growth in the economy spurred by the nation's scientific effort has had and will continue to have a great impact on the financial world. The nation has been sold on scientific research, and perhaps if really good basic research was done in the financial world the country would be enthusiastic about it. Maybe basic financial research is where scientific research was in the thirties and before the war. Corporations then had to be persuaded to adopt applied scientific and technological research. Few companies were prepared to undertake scientific, logical, or systematic development of new products, processes, and techniques. By 1950 the trend had changed completely, and scientific research was something every company had to do.

Similarly, by 1950 the need for applied scientific research was beginning to diminish, and the need for economic studies began to appear. Emphasis was then placed on techno-economic research. Recently an executive of one of the leading industrial companies stated: "Industry must spend on research in the social sciences, of which marketing is a part, as much as is being spent on the physical sciences." Marketing research, incidentally, profits somewhat from about $18 billion spent each year on advertising.

Today many companies are coordinating their economic studies, their economic planning, and their scientific research work. Out of such techno-economic research teams, research know-how is developing in the industrial field in companies such as duPont and in institutions such as Stanford Research, but so far little work of this nature is being done in the financial world – a field where it is really needed.

It is said that scientific research encompasses such a wide field – "obscure chemical reactions, subtle biological processes, invisible electrical phenomena, and elusive kinetic forces" – that no single company can master all the techniques, let alone apply them to industrial uses. Basic research in certain areas in the financial world may not be any less difficult. It may be even more complicated.

One hears a great deal about the limited number of scientists, but it appears that good social *scientists* are even scarcer. In a recent article in the New York *Times* Myrdal quoted Oxenstierna, who was Chancellor to King Gustavus Adolphus, as saying, "My son, my son, if you knew with what little wisdom the world is ruled." Wisdom is still a rare article today.

There are many Luddites in the financial business, as there are in all industries, and about the only way to get them to move forward is by selling them on the need for innovations that can be developed through basic research. This is not going to be easy. The American Institute of Certified Public Accountants, for example, has just issued a report, *The CPA Plans for the Future,* which stresses the need for more basic research. The report says that it took the Institute's Committee on Long-Range Objectives nine years of effort to isolate and identify the problems outlined in the report. The report is well worth checking for ideas for financial research projects.

It is to be hoped that the sponsorship of this symposium by the University of Virginia Graduate School of Business Administration will encourage a number of progressive financial institutions to undertake or support specific research projects. The results achieved should demonstrate how very worth while good basic research can be.

The Financial Process, Financial Institutions, and Financial Services

Charles C. Abbott
Dean
Graduate School of Business Administration
University of Virginia

THIS memorandum addresses itself to three questions, more appropriate to basic than to applied research and at the present time specially cogent:

1. By what standards should "the financial process" in the United States be judged in 1965?

2. Why is this an especially important question at the present time?

3. Why has the enormous amount of financial research done during the last generation or two not provided comprehensive and generally accepted answers to these questions?

Obviously, a short and informal memorandum of this type cannot give definitive answers. If it raises a few of the right questions, it will have served its purpose.

The Financial Process

First let us define our terms. "Financial process" as here employed means the transfer of funds from the points in the economy where they are saved, accumulated, or created to the points in the economy where they are employed. Clearly the process involves most if not all types of financial institutions. While the concept is analogous to economists' "savings and investment" process, it is not precisely the same thing.

A few examples will make plain some of the differences. Savings and reinvestment done by individual business concerns, most important in the "savings and investment" process, are excluded from the "financial process" as here defined, since the sums involved are not transferred. Some of the funds shifted from one pair of hands to another in the financial process, such as the proceeds of bank loans or perhaps even open account credit, are not "savings" as usually defined. Some of the uses to which funds received through the transfer process – whether savings or not – are not "investment" in the usual sense of economists, though they are in the parlance of businessmen and financial people, for example, the purchase for cash of a company's assets by another company. This is not "investment" in the economic sense, through it would normally be so described by the merging company. Another case is the purchase of existing securities by pension funds, banks, investment companies, insurance companies, and the whole range of financial intermediaries.

Financial institutions and organized security markets are an integral and essential part of this process. As such, they are service organizations and form part of the service trades. They do not themselves produce anything tangible, as do the manufacturing and extractive industries. It is in this context of the services they provide that they must be evaluated, a point to be explored more fully further on.

The fact that the financial process and the structure of financial institutions permit individuals and companies to transfer funds from the places where they are saved to where they can be employed makes wealth far more liquid than would otherwise be the case. This liquidity aids enormously in the ongoing and never-ceasing solution of the basic economic problem – the allocation of scarce resources among infinite ends; it aids in rationing credit and capital among the almost infinite number of claimants and claimant needs that make up both the public and private sectors of the economy. Such allocation, taking place through financial markets, has made great contributions to the economic development of the United States. Similarly, the liquidity given wealth by the transfer process is probably the first essential condition for the evolution and growth of capital markets.

Here is not the place to explore the importance of the financial process, the liquidity of wealth, and the growth of capital markets for underdeveloped countries. But it may be ventured that if these countries do not find ways to create their own transfer process and capital markets, they are not likely to become economically independent of the United States, Western Europe, or the Communist bloc.

By What Standards Should the Financial Process Be Judged?

The financial process should be judged by how effectively it aids the attainment of national economic objectives and by how efficiently and cheaply it provides the full complement of services that persons, governmental units, and business concerns can reasonably expect from it. In short, it serves two masters. If it serves both well, presumably it will also provide the flexibility in the economy and the encouragement to private enterprise that are, perhaps, the ultimate standards against which the financial structure and its operation should be assessed.

The last thirty years have seen considerable variation and evolution in national economic goals. Stabilization of the business cycle, stabilization of the price level, stability for the monetary unit on the foreign exchanges, creation of a favorable or elimination of an unfavorable balance of payments, reduction of unemployment, maintenance of employment at some predetermined level of the work force, maintenance of a degree of military power adequate for national security, achievement of economic growth at some set percentage of the GNP, are only some of the purposes that have been suggested. Whether some or all are mutually compatible is another question.

Determination of which of these objectives should have priority is clearly not a task for research in *finance*. But when and as a consensus develops, basic as well as applied research will have a series of tasks in determining the best means to achieve the desired ends.

The range of financial services required to satisfy the legitimate needs of persons, governmental units, and business concerns has expanded enormously during the last generation.

Predictably the next thirty years will witness an equal or larger growth. For example, the period since the Great Depression has seen the increase of common trust funds, mutual funds, and the "third market," the Farm Credit Administration and the Home Loan Bank System, and the proliferation of different kinds of savings arrangements; it has witnessed the evolution of a host of new types of lending that range from consumer credit to term loans and private placements; it has experienced the extension of checking accounts and other financial services to large segments of the population theretofore not directly served by the financial world.

These developments notwithstanding, we do not really know whether the range and structure of services offered by financial institutions and markets make the maximum possible contribution to "satisfactory" performance of the economy as a whole; nor do we really know whether the array and structure of services offered by financial institutions to individuals are adequate to satisfy the latter's needs and desires. Much less do we have the answer to this question for the years ahead. In view of the changes during the last generation the supposition is that we do not.

Were documentation of these statements needed, questions indicating the extent of our ignorance abound. We have some knowledge of the volume of "saving" and "investment" required to support one or more of the types of performance desired of the national economy, but we have very little knowledge of how best to combine "internal" and "external" investment by business concerns in order that our goals may be achieved. Furthermore, what *are* – let alone what *should be* – the relations and the proportionate significance, dollar-wise, of the national capital markets and the regional and local capital markets that exist in every population center of 25,000 persons or over? Economic literature is largely silent.

Even if we knew with precision the aggregates of "savings" and "investment" necessary to achieve national objectives, over-all figures would not tell us how savings seeking investment should be constituted as between "trustee money" and "sporty money" and all the intermediate kinds of investment funds. "Savings money" is no more homogeneous than are "investment opportunities," and we do not know under what circumstances financial institutions and capital markets will offer the requisite mix of investment possibilities in small business and big business, in common stocks and AAA bonds, in "income securities" and "capital appreciation" securities that, on the one hand, will accomplish our objectives and, on the other hand, furnish persons, business concerns, and governmental units with the range and type of services they may legitimately expect. And finally, what is or should be the relation of the new issue market – crucially important in both theory and practice – to national economic objectives?

To go no further back than 1930, evidence has suggested several times that the demand for "trustee investments" exceeded the new supply of such paper and that the demand for "risk capital" exceeded the volume of funds of this type available for investment. It hardly needs to be added that, in terms of some national objective such as "full employment," an imbalance between the supply of different kinds of funds seeking investment and the need or demands of the economy for "sporty" or "trustee money" can create conditions virtually as serious as an imbalance between global savings and investment figures. One of the few things that we do know is that a high-level economy cannot long be operated if, on the one hand, there is "too much" speculation or, on the other hand, only blue ribbon risks and trustee investments can get takers.

Appraisal of the financial process may also be made in terms of particular types of credit, capital, and services. During the past generation the volume of funds offered American agriculture – both credit and capital – has been excessive, virtually without regard for what national objective is selected. Many people have felt that in terms of national welfare the flow of equity money and of credit into small businesses has been deficient, certainly in terms of over-all economic goals. From time to time, sometimes for considerable periods, the capital markets for one reason or another have not been "open" for business financing, and sometimes for years on end some essential industries such as banks and railroads either have not been able to raise new money or have been able only on such onerous terms as were prohibitive. Industrial mortgage money has, at least at times, been notoriously difficult to obtain. It is not clear whether commercial banks, particularly small to medium-size banks, do or do not furnish the mix of services most needed by their communities. It can be plausibly argued that had the insurance industry been more alert to public desires and the profit possibilities inherent in them, the federal government would not be so heavily involved in the variety of security programs with which it is now concerned. The enormous growth of consumer credit in its multifarious forms suggests that for a long time there was a demand for this type of service not satisfied by the then existing structure of institutions. Again, it can be shown that virtually no attention has been given by private financial institutions to the needs of the small man in property management and estate planning—though this situation seems to be rapidly changing.

Finally, the great revolution in the structure of financial institutions we are now witnessing is in itself evidence that persons in the financial world recognize that the present organizational framework may not be ideally designed either to provide the services the public wishes or to exploit the profit opportunities in them. Commercial banks are increasingly seeking to widen their scope and their services through merger, the establishment of branches, and the formation of holding companies; and there is much concern regarding competitive equality as between national and state-chartered institutions. Mutual funds and insurance companies are each invading territory long viewed as the preserve of the other. Investment banking houses are concerned with their long-run future and are studying new fields in which their specialized knowledge can be profitably employed. The concept of "financial department stores" that will offer all the services the typical family or business concern will need from the cradle to the grave comes closer to reality – if only it could be determined what these services during the next thirty years will in fact be! Financial regulatory authorities of all types are increasingly concerned with redefining their responsibilities and are embroiled with each other concerning their proper mandates. In short, simple observation suggests that we may not have the "proper" framework of regulation to further national purposes – whatever these may be determined to be.

The Importance of Standards

The financial process, capital formation, and capital markets are at the very heart of the type of free enterprise system that has brought this country to its present high pitch of development. But many aspects of the process are not well understood, and we do not know with precision how all of the parts of the process and of capital markets do in fact fit together and operate, let alone how they *should* function in order that the structure of financial institutions may fulfill its responsibilities most advantageously. Many, perhaps most, financial institutions do not have a careful, systematic, and reasoned rationale of the services that they are – and are not – providing; this defect in considerable degree is paralleled by the absence of standards for evaluating the performance of the financial structure as a whole.

The form of economic organization in the United States, with its great reliance on free markets, is currently in competition with and under criticism from other types of organizations that do not depend on the market as the guide for the production and distribution of goods and services. It may well be that our lack of more exact comprehension of some of the essentials of our system enhances the vulnerability of this country to such attacks. Furthermore, the financial framework in the United States is itself in the midst of a very rapid evolution. In the absence of better measures of performance than we now have it is not clear whether all of the actual or suggested changes are in fact steps forward or back.

One thing, however, has been made abundantly clear by the financial history of the last generation. If the private institutions that constitute the bulk of the money and capital markets and conduct the major portion of financial business do not perform "satisfactorily" in terms of national economic objectives and – perhaps even more important – do not offer the range, structure, and variety of services the country and their customers need, one or both of two results follow: (*a*) private institutions will be "regulated" by public authority with a view to improving their performance; (b) new institutions, created or at least fostered by public authority, will be injected into the structure to supply services the public demands.

Conclusion

Financial institutions continuously conduct an enormous amount of research, most of which quite properly is directed at discovering profit possibilities in the current scene or the near-term future and must be characterized as applied research. Such efforts are generally not directed at answering questions of the type raised in this memorandum nor focused on the role of the institution in the larger framework of which it is a part. Much of what may be loosely called "academic financial research" either has a historical approach and is concerned with analyzing what has happened in the past or studies the economy primarily from the point of view of the monetary theory as contrasted with the needs of the customers. The chief public investigations of the country's financial system have generally been undertaken subsequent to some scandal or serious breakdown in the mechanism. Such inquiries have necessarily had as their point of departure the correction of specific abuses. Essential as is "reform," studies concerned with remedying particular deficiencies can hardly be expected to take a broad, speculative approach designed to formulate hypotheses and standards of how the financial process should work if it is to serve the public and the economy to best advantage.

In summary, what this memorandum has attempted to say is that there has not been a thorough, systematic, and comprehensive study of the framework of financial institutions in the United States and the range of services that they individually and collectively offer; there has not been a careful attempt to relate the structure of financial services to the needs of people, individual localities, or the country as a whole; and – even more important for the years ahead – there is no thoroughgoing and generally accepted set of standards for measuring satisfactory performance on the part of the financial process and the structure of the financial institution. Since this process and the capital markets are the center of the type of free enterprise economy that has brought the United States to its present stage, this lack is of special importance when this country's economic system is being challenged by others that are both competitive and hostile.

The Need for Basic Research in the Field of Finance

Blake T. Newton
President
Institute of Life Insurance
Life Insurance Association of America

James J. O'Leary
Vice President and Director of Economic Research
Institute of Life Insurance
Life Insurance Association of America

FOR THE past two decades the life insurance business has recognized the desirability of a stronger basic research effort in the field of finance. During this period the life insurance business has sponsored a program which has two facets: *(a)* to develop a comprehensive body of useful data with respect to the functioning of life insurance companies as financial institutions and *(b)* to sponsor, through research grants to universities and private research bureaus, basic research in the money and capital markets. The *1964 Record of Life Insurance Investments,* which is condensed in Appendix A, reviews the investment research program of the life insurance business. This covers both the research done by the LIAA staff as well as the research projects which have been financed. During the last two decades the life insurance business has made grants of approximately $2 million for basic research in the area of finance. Most of these projects, we believe, definitely fit the description of the research indicated in Dean Abbott's letter.

At the same time, however, we recognize that the research sponsored by the life insurance business has met only a small part of the need. Other institutions functioning in the money and capital markets have not followed our lead to any great extent in providing funds for basic research. There are indications that the American Bankers Association may be starting a program to provide financing for basic research, but in general the work which has been done by other types of financial institutions has been rather narrowly pointed toward industry matters. The American financial system is changing rapidly. Old problems are disappearing and new ones are emerging. Financial institutions are in a process of continual change, as are investment policies. Real understanding of our financial system on the part of congressmen, public officials, the academic community, and the general public is meager.

Because of our continuing interest in basic research in the field of finance the Investment Research Committee of the LIAA in 1963 invited the National Bureau of Economic Research to undertake an exploratory study of research needs in the capital markets. The NBER appointed a committee to guide this study, the results of which were published in the May 1964 Supplement to Volume XIX of the *Journal of Finance.**

We believe that the report of the NBER Exploratory Committee contains a number of valuable suggestions for basic research in areas which should be of real interest to the group headed by Dean Abbott. The list of projects suggested by the Committee is by no means exhaustive, and we are supplementing it at the end of this memorandum. First, however, it is in order to give an appraisal of the ideas and some of the projects set forth in the NBER report. We agree with the thought expressed in the report that a great deal of progress has been made in the past two decades in filling in gaps in our knowledge about the behavior of financial institutions and about the functioning of our financial system in general. Our system is rapidly changing; hence the job of keeping abreast of developments is a never-ending one. We believe, however, that the time has come when the nature of the research carried out should be more interpretive and analytical; that is, there should be a shift to analyzing the behavior of our financial system in the light of the

---

*For a summarization of this document see Appendix B.

wealth of data we have accumulated. Moreover, we believe that new research in this area should be directed more toward illuminating the major economic issues encountered in the formulation and execution of public policy.

Part II of the NBER report presents a number of recommendations for further research on the capital market as a whole. We believe that it would be very fruitful to undertake a study designed to determine how the money and capital markets either hinder or facilitate the attainment of such national economic growth, price stability, high-level employment, efficient allocation of resources, and balance of payments equilibrium. The existing body of information should make such an analytical study worth while. The idea of a study that would draw up projections of savings, investments, and flows of funds from ultimate lenders – directly or through financial institutions – to ultimate borrowers over the next decade or two in the United States has a great deal of appeal to us. The work done by Kuznets, which was supported by a grant from the life insurance business and published a few years ago, should be updated in the light of the changes which have occurred in our economy. We think that there is also merit in the proposal for a study of the role of government in the capital markets, as well as of the interrelations among various sectors of the capital market.

Clearly valuable research can be conducted on the subject of the influence of financial markets on real expenditures. For example, it is widely held that a rise of long-term interest rates restricts the rate of capital spending. But is this true? To what extent do movements of interest rates – up or down – have an effect on capital spending by business and industry or on residential construction? To what extent do interest rate changes affect the rate of saving? These questions will be explored in the Interest Rate Study currently being conducted by the NBER with the aid of a grant from LIAA, but we are sure that there is plenty of room for additional research on this broad subject.

Similarly, we agree with the NBER report that a more intensive study of the quality of credit – the forces affecting the quality of credit, the trends, and cyclical aspects – would contribute significantly to a better understanding of our financial system. It would also help to point the way to sound public policy affecting the quality of credit.

Part III of the NBER report also contains a number of worth-while suggestions for research on particular sectors of the capital market. Most of them, however, are in the nature of research designed to fill gaps in our knowledge of the functioning of our financial system. In the NBER Interest Rate Study we hope that a comprehensive body of information will be developed on the market for multifamily and commercial mortgages. The area which we think has real promise, in the light of the objectives set forth in Dean Abbott's letter, is the market for federal government securities. During the past fifteen years there have been highly significant changes in the attitudes of institutional investors toward government securities, especially long-term bonds. It would be profitable to explore these changes and to analyze the implications for Treasury debt management. The study might ask such questions as: (a) Can federal debt management be employed effectively as a counter-cyclical device? (b) When should the Treasury seek to sell long-term bonds? (c) Even if the interest ceiling on long-term government bonds is removed or raised, can the United States Treasury compete effectively for long-term funds under current and foreseeable market conditions?

Finally, there are three areas of research which we would like to suggest to supplement the NBER report. First, there have been vitally important changes in the commercial banking system, especially during the past five years. During this time the loans and investments of the banks have expanded without a corresponding increase in demand deposits. We have had the development of CD's and the issuance of notes by banks in order to obtain funds for loans and investments. Similarly, there have been important changes in nonbank institutions. The question which would be interesting to explore is how such changes in the financial system have affected the power of the FRS to control the money supply.

Closely related to the foregoing would be a study focused directly on the following question: To what extent is the great expansion of time deposits in commercial banks the product of saving versus credit creation by the banks on the basis of fractional reserves? It is argued by some, for example, that commercial banks have created demand deposits but that the amendments to Regulation Q have promoted a continuous shifting of demand deposits into the time deposit category.

Another question which might be explored is the changing risk preferences of institutional investors. During the past fifteen or twenty years institutional investors, as a matter of policy, have been willing to assume increasing risks in their investments–at least what appear by some standards to be increasing risks. For example, whereas twenty years ago it was normal for institutions to limit themselves to conventional mortgage loans not in excess of two-thirds of the value of the property, today the amount is 75 percent or higher. This study could accumulate the facts about the move toward greater risk preference, the forces behind it, and the implications for public and private policy.

In conclusion, we would like to do everything possible to encourage Dean Abbott and his colleagues in their thinking about basic research in finance.

Memorandum

Orson H. Hart
Second Vice President
Economic Research Division
New York Life Insurance Company

DEAN ABBOTT'S suggestion that we give some thought to the basic functions of the financial world should serve to remind us that when business institutions fail to perform a useful purpose in the general economy they lose their reason for being, and in due course they pass into a footnote on the pages of history. The financial world today is a vigorous sector of our economy; certainly there is no reason to believe that it is not essential to the over-all system. The scope of its activities is, however, undergoing fundamental changes, and I agree that it is time to examine some of its functions, particularly when business and financial changes are occurring as rapidly as they are today.

Over the years that I have been employed in financial work, I have been impressed by the lack of clear definition of the capital market and the functions it is supposed to perform. Just in passing, I wonder how many of the group among whom these papers are being circulated are satisfied that they understand the principal ramifications of the organized stock market on the national economy? I would like to know more about the monetary income that is created and destroyed by the rapid changes in stock prices and how these adjustments in income are offset, if they are offset, by monetary and/or fiscal policy.

The financial area in which I think some basic reflection would be most rewarding, however, concerns the flow of funds into and out of the capital market through commercial banks. The expansion of commercial bank assets since 1960 is approaching $100 billion, an amount almost three times the assets of the entire system in 1929. It must be remembered that this expansion has occurred in a period of peace and cyclical prosperity when one would have expected credit restraint to become increasingly severe and the rate of bank asset expansion to decline. Indeed, such factors as the outflow of gold and the related balance of payments difficulties, the rising utilization of plant capacity, and the decline in unemployment – all would lead you to expect a progressively less liberal reserve policy on the part of the central banking system. Such has not been the case, however. Reserves have risen at an annual rate of 4 percent since the end of 1959, while bank asset expansion has proceeded at an annual rate of well over 7 percent.

Notwithstanding this very liberal credit policy, the economy does not seem to have become inflated. Indeed, the rise in the consumer price index has probably not been a great deal more since 1960 than the gains in quality in many consumer items. A number of such items, moreover, are lower in price, as for example, color television, now a very substantial volume item in the appliance field. Certain other prices also have declined including cocoa, various man-made fibers such as nylon and dacron, and many plastics and other chemicals. Automobile owners today can buy Prestone and other quality antifreezes for approximately half the price they paid in 1960.

This relative stability of prices in the face of a rapid expansion of bank credit and other stimulating government policies has led a number of monetary economists to conclude that a substantial proportion of the asset expansion of commercial banks can be traced to the banks' competitive ability to attract savings vis-à-vis other financial institutions. But others argue that with few exceptions funds can flow into the commercial banking system only as a reflection of loan or investment expansion, and that the present expansion, therefore, is credit creation in the usual sense. Clearly this is a basic controversy. If the first school is right, the commercial banks today are mobilizing savings, and their activities may be largely neutral as far as the expansion of the economy is concerned. If the second is right, they are creating credit on a major scale, and their activities are clearly expansionary and may be inflationary under present conditions.

I shall not attempt to inquire much further into the question in this paper, but perhaps a few observations about capital flows through commercial banks will serve to arouse the interest of some of the people who are engaged in this exchange of ideas. I assume one commercial bank, i.e., a system analysis, in the following discussion.

When the mutual savings banks and the savings and loan associations gain funds, the gains come about through deposits or share purchases, through borrowings, or through the earnings of the institutions. The flow may therefore be visualized as entering one of these institutions through a liability or surplus account and passing out of the institution when the funds are invested. A rise in liabilities and/or surplus leads to a rise in assets; the funds are externally, not internally, generated.

In the case of commercial banks – I am talking about the system, as noted above – the course of events is just the reverse. A rise in loans and/or investments leads to a rise in deposits, whether the deposits are demand deposits, savings deposits, or other time deposits. Only through certain limited avenues, such as a decline in money in circulation, can deposits rise first, and this would seem to say that the commercial banking system cannot collect savings and then invest them, as the conventional savings institutions do, without some liability offset.

So now I ask, is this so? If it is so, does it mean that a rise in the savings or time accounts of commercial banks has to be offset by a decline in demand deposits, other things remaining equal? Or to go back to my original question, is all the deposit expansion of commercial banks of the same order and basically different from the deposit expansion of savings institutions, or are the savings accounts of commercial banks, and possibly other time accounts, of the same general character as the savings deposits of the savings institutions?

It seems to me that these are basic questions concerning the expansionary role of the commercial banking system in the over-all economy. For if it is true that all deposit expansion of commercial banks is basically credit creation, our present monetary policy surely must be judged as highly stimulative, hardly providing any check on either the public or the private sector. But if it is not true, the commercial banks may be collecting and investing a rising volume of savings, a process with quite different economic implications.

PART III

Functioning of the Capital Markets

Commentary

INEVITABLY a deficiency of logic or a lack of equity pervades any attempt to put contributions to a symposium in some sort of order. Such is particularly the case in this collection, and nowhere perhaps is the problem more evident than in Part III. Many of the topics touched on in the papers grouped here are the same as topics dealt with in memoranda placed under other headings, and many of the subjects commented on elsewhere in this volume are identical with some of those mentioned here. Nevertheless, by selecting questions from the papers in this section and placing them in juxtaposition, it is, perhaps, possible to develop a useful continuance of thought, even though such a continuance does substantial injustice to the contributors by minimizing the range and variety of the considerations with which they have dealt.

> Obviously ... we must take action based on where we are at present, that is, based on the financial system as it now exists.

> .   .   .   .   .

> If one's concern is with optimal behavior, then it is clear that we must have three kinds of knowledge. First, we must know our goal – that is, we must have a model or conception of what optimal behavior of financial markets really is. Second, we must know how far the existing system is from this optimal position. And, third, we must know what steps we must take in order to bring the existing system closer to the optimum, which involves knowing why the existing system deviates from this optimum. – Giles Mellon

> Unless we have a clear-cut understanding of the relationship between business objectives and the cost of capital, the entire idea underlying the efficiency of a private enterprise system evaporates. – Ezra Solomon

More forward-looking research might be undertaken in the relationship of the performance of the
several types of financial institutions in business cycle
swings.

.   .   .   .   .

If a recession seems to be coming, that may be
exactly the time to increase and sharpen the efforts of
individuals and businesses so that the effect of the recession can be lessened. This in effect means compensatory action from private sources, rather than dependence upon the government. – Charles Moeller, Jr.

The second area of interest has to do with the dissection of
these institutional changes and the accommodation of the new
relationships within the existing body of economic knowledge
and theory, primarily by integrating these data with national
product and income accounts, input-output analysis, flow-of-
funds constructs, and corporate sources and uses of funds. In
the case of no other topic in the symposium, perhaps, is there
such a clear-cut consensus regarding the need for basic research.
W. Giles Mellon, Charles Moeller, Jr., Blake T. Newton
and James J. O'Leary, Carlton R. Copp, and C. Stewart
Sheppard, among others, deal with this; the last two restrict
their contributions to this single topic.

Just as there is a concentration of interest in further investigation of flow-of-funds analysis, so is there considerable consensus on what might be achieved by such research, both in the
area of forecasting and in improvement in the economy's efficiency.

It would seem desirable to have a fairly long-term
projection of what the financial system might conceivably expect in the way of inflows of funds and demands
for credit. . . .

By pinpointing possible future problems, such a
projection could serve as a guide to the way in which
the financial system should be changed. – W. Giles
Mellon

Specifically, the formulation of the determinants of
interest rates is highly important. . . . The spending

decisions that comprise and create GNP must be related to the investment policies and practices of financial institutions, as well as with monetary and fiscal policies. When such relationships are established, the forecasting of changes in the various supply and demand factors should be feasible. – Charles Moeller, Jr.

There exist the specific challenges to relate flow of funds to corporate sources and uses of funds, to business fluctuations, and to interest rate changes. – C. Stewart Sheppard

Using this framework of the sources and uses of short-term and investment funds, it would then be possible to measure the *relative cost effectiveness* of the various financial institutions. . . .

A useful supplementary research area might be the comparison and ranking of all financial intermediaries on the basis of cost and return of capital, perhaps starting with the government, banks, and prime borrowers, and ending with the marginal commercial, financial, or brokerage-type operations. – Carlton R. Copp

From this array of observations one tentative conclusion may be drawn. Real comprehension of the revolution in the financial structure now in process is not likely to be achieved either by a purely statistical approach or by a study that restricts itself to organizational changes. A combination of both will be required.

Basic Financial Research

W. Giles Mellon
Financial Economist
The Chase Manhattan Bank

UNTIL very recently, the area of finance and financial institutions was relatively neglected by serious economic research; it lacked both essential data and theoretical explanations. In the last few years, however, the attention of economists has focused more and more on the financial sector. In the collection of data NBER and the Flow-of-Funds Division of the Federal Reserve have made notable contributions. At the same time theoretical economists have made major advances in studying the demand and supply of money, portfolio adjustment progress, optimal investment patterns, the structure of interest rates, and other such topics. Moreover, research activity in the field of finance seems to be accelerating, with joint projects at Yale, Harvard, Princeton, Chicago, Carnegie Tech, and the National Bureau now active. In addition, a large number of individuals are conducting studies.

This research has, in the main, been directed toward explanation and prediction of the existing financial system. Although some attention has been paid to possible reform, especially in the area of monetary policy, optimal behavior has, in general, entered only in attempts to establish rules for profit maximization for the individual firm operating within the boundaries of the existing system.

What Messrs. Abbott, Boushall, Harding, Hart, and Roehl are proposing is an extension in research on optimal behavior to include the financial system as a whole. They are interested in such topics as the proper relationship between the private financial markets and regulatory agencies, the way in which the financial markets *should* be organized to serve the public best, and so on. Thus, while such research would obviously overlap with, and rely upon, much of the research previously conducted in the financial area – as, for example, the work done in connection with the *Report of the Commission on Money and Credit* – its general direction and orientation would be unique.

There is little doubt that such a program of research would be valuable and would fill a real need in the financial area – if it can be carried out in an effective manner. In the following paragraphs I have outlined briefly certain general areas that I think should be explored in a study of this type.

SPECIFIC RESEARCH SUGGESTIONS

If one's concern is with optimal behavior, then it is clear that we must have three kinds of knowledge. First, we must know our goal – that is, we must have a model or conception of what optimal behavior of financial markets really is. Second, we must know how far the existing system is from this optimal position. And, third, we must know what steps we must take in order to bring the existing system closer to the optimum, which involves knowing why the existing system deviates from this optimum. This means, in turn, that a program of investigation can be divided into two related parts.

1. *Model of Optimal Financial System.* An interesting project would be to turn a group of research economists loose on the problem of designing a perfect economic-financial system from scratch. What type of institutions would such a system include, how would they be regulated, what services could they offer, how would monetary and fiscal policy be integrated into the system, how would we allow for the effect of international financial interrelationships, and so on?

2. *Improving Our Existing System.* Obviously, however, we must take action based on where we are at present, that is, based on the financial system as it now exists. The key problems in a research program such as the authors of the memorandum contemplate would be to isolate the major areas where our existing financial system deviates from the ideal and to prescribe rules for reasonable improvement, using the ideal as a guide but realizing fully that human nature and extant eco-

nomic knowledge will never permit us to reach that ideal. Such a program of research could cover an almost unlimited range of subjects. Some specific suggestions for possible first steps are contained in the following sections.

I. Survey of Relevant Research

A logical first point of departure would be to sponsor a project to survey all extant research in the financial area which is relevant to the question of how the financial system might be reformed. This material is currently widely scattered in economic and business literature, and its collection and summarization would be a great service to economists. It would, moreover, reveal just what the gaps are in our existing knowledge of the financial system.

II. Projection of Expected Future Demands

Along with a summary of existing research as a guide to the over-all project, it would seem desirable to have a fairly long-term projection of what the financial system might conceivably expect in the way of inflows of funds and demands for credit. This should, in my opinion, take the form of a formal long-term projection of flows of funds based on a formal model of the economy and its financial subsectors. No such long-range projections in the financial area now exist, although there are any number of long-term projections of the general economy.

By pinpointing possible future problems, such a projection could serve as a guide to the way in which the financial system should be changed. A projected shortage of consumer credit at satisfactory interest rates, for example, might suggest the need to relax restrictions on financial institutions which are now not permitted to operate in the consumer credit area, and so on.

III. A Survey of Consumer and Business Needs

Since the main aim of the over-all project is to study how the financial community may better meet the needs of business and the public, in addition to a more or less formal projection of expected demands on the financial community, a worth-while project might be a scientific survey of consumers and business.

This, if well done, could give useful indications of ways these segments of the economy feel existing financial services might be improved and the new services which they think should be offered.

IV. The Movement of the Deviation from the Optimal System over Time

A topic which would be of interest to economists with a historical bent and which overlaps some of the other possible areas of research would be an attempt to determine whether or not the United States financial system has been moving closer to an optimal position over time in various areas.

V. Conflicts between National and International Financial Systems

An important subject to be considered would be whether or not there are inherent conflicts between the attempts of various countries to improve their domestic financial systems. If so, what international organization and rules should be established to reconcile these conflicting objectives?

VI. Study of the Actual Effect of Existing Restrictions on the Activities of Financial Institutions

A topic which I have never seen explored in sufficient detail is the effect on the economy and financial markets of the numerous restrictions which are imposed by various governmental bodies on the activities of financial institutions. Commercial banks, for example, cannot engage in certain activities, cannot branch outside certain areas, and cannot invest in certain types of securities. In some states insurance companies can invest in common stock with greater freedom than in others. Mutual savings banks cannot make consumer credit loans, and so on. In addition, there is the whole question of the effect of differential taxation.

As a general rule, on a purely profit maximization basis, elimination of an existing constraint on economic action can never make an institution or individual worse off; probably it will allow improvement of an existing economic position. But there are two additional considerations. The first is that there may be good and sufficient reasons for deviation from the rule of full freedom in financial activities. The rules of the SEC, FRS, state banking boards, and the like were, after all, not adopted in a vacuum, but in response to real abuses in the financial system. Perhaps these abuses no longer exist or are guarded against by other reforms; e.g., adequate bank examination may be a sufficient protection to bank depositors to render unnecessary any restrictions on the type of securities in which banks may invest. This type of problem should, however, be carefully studied before any relaxation in restrictions is advocated.

Second, it is realistic to try to reach at least some quasi-quantitative measure of just how much damage is done by each of these restrictions. For example, there is certainly not complete freedom of entry into the business of being a government securities dealer, yet that market seems to operate efficiently and probably would not be improved to any significant degree by allowing another one hundred firms to enter the business. On the other hand, the restriction which allows a state pension fund to invest only in government or state and local securities is almost surely harmful to the employees covered, and its removal would broaden the markets in which the funds could be placed. It is reasonable, therefore, to examine all these restrictions in turn and to concentrate attention on removing those which do the most harm.

VII. Study on Removable and Inherent Friction in Financial Markets

Even if all restrictions of a legal nature are removed or if the best possible set of legal restrictions is imposed, the financial system will still not be perfect. Adjustments will take time to make, information will not be perfect, individuals and institutions will make errors of judgment.

Certain of these limitations may be inherent in the financial system – as, for example, time lags in the effect of monetary policy – though probably even here their efforts could be reduced by making structural changes in the system. Other limitations, however, can be removed. As an example, there is the question of information. An interesting study could be made of the gaps in our present statistical information which prevent optimal decisions by consumers and businesses and by the federal government and the FRS, and on the best method to fill these gaps.

CONCLUDING REMARKS

A study of this type, though it would incorporate certain very concrete elements, is nevertheless bound to be in a sense less rigorous than, say, a statistical investigation of a particular financial market because of the inevitable inclusion of value judgments. Because this is true, the persons directing the project would have to exercise extreme care in two respects. One, they would have to include the widest possible points of view in the participants selected. And, two, since it would be easy to drift into not very helpful generalities, care would have to be taken to keep the entire discussion on as rigorous a basis as possible. If these guiding principles can be followed, then I think that there would be a very good chance of developing a useful and unique research effort in this area.

Memorandum regarding Desirable Basic Research in Finance

Ezra Solomon
Dean Witter Professor of Finance
Graduate School of Business
Stanford University

ALTHOUGH my suggestion does not deal primarily and directly with financial institutions, I think it is sufficiently important to warrant inclusion in an inventory of desired research.

We need much more speculative thinking and analysis and, hopefully, some measurement regarding the *cost of capital* concept and the relation of the magnitude of cost of capital to events in the financial markets.

In particular:

1. Unless we have a clear-cut understanding of the relationship between business objectives and the cost of capital, the entire idea underlying the efficiency of a private enterprise system evaporates.

2. We need some thinking about the cost of capital and its use in the regulation of public utilities. With the inclusion of natural gas among regulated enterprises, the power of regulatory commissions is even larger than it used to be; and, again, unless we have some clear-cut concepts on the cost of capital to regulated industries, we are unlikely to get intelligent performance from the regulators.

3. Finally, the best long-run safeguard of an economy in which public sector investment takes a rising share of capital formation is an understanding of the role that ought to be played by a defensible cost of capital measure in the allocation of social resources.

The Declining Role of the Investment Banker in Corporation Finance

Bion B. Howard
Nathan and Mary Sharp Professor of Finance
School of Business, Northwestern University

THE investment banker in his traditional role of underwriter and marketer of new security issues is playing a lesser and lesser part in financing United States industry. Is this a trend that is likely to continue? What changes have already occurred and are now occurring in the private sector of the economy and in the pattern of savings which are contributing to the decline in need for investment banking services? Are they likely to persist? Are there areas not now served, or inadequately served, where the investment banker might play an enlarged role? What institutional changes might best foster this growth?

QUESTIONS FOR STUDY

1. Is the growth of corporate assets keeping pace with the economy – with the GNP?
    a. Does increased efficiency in business result in more goods and services produced per dollar of asset investment?
    b. Or is greater automation leading to greater asset investment per dollar of output?
    c. Is there a trend in demand for goods and services to industries requiring comparatively smaller asset investment?
2. What has been the trend of internal versus external financing? What are the background factors which might lead to changes in the current proportions?
3. What factors have contributed to the relative growth of private placement of new corporate securities? Are they likely to persist or accentuate the trend?

4. With a growing concentration of business in larger "blue chip" companies, is it likely that a greater percentage of privileged subscription offerings will not be underwritten as in the AT & T situation?

5. Is a greater segment of the business of the country being concentrated in large publicly held companies? If so, they are better able to finance growth through retained earnings or private placement of debt securities, hence reducing the need for public financing.

6. What are the trends in intercorporate financing? Is there a growth in down-stream financing through accounts payable, installment notes, and lease to smaller companies by large ones?

7. Will the changing mix of bank deposits lead to an even greater proportion of term loan financing by banks and hence less need for public sale of securities?

8. Will the present rising trend of industrial municipal financing continue?

9. Examine the changes in patterns of savings and the changes in growth and function of savings institutions – other than those discussed in the questions above – for their bearing on increased competition in the direct financing of private business.

POSSIBLE AREAS OF INCREASED ACTIVITY

1. Assumption of governmental financing and guarantee of activities.

2. Small business.

3. International and foreign business.

Some Areas for Basic Research, Particularly regarding Financial Institutions

Charles Moeller, Jr.
Economist
Metropolitan Life Insurance Company

ALTHOUGH this memorandum attempts to outline some areas of basic research that might be explored, it in no way minimizes the considerable amount of research, both basic and applied, that has been undertaken during the past twenty years in the field of finance.

Unfortunately, the National Science Foundation does not include economics and other social sciences in its compilation of research and development outlays. However, if the growth in funds devoted to the social sciences were included, it would undoubtedly compare importantly with the sharp expansions now shown in the National Science Foundation series.

In light of the fact that the distinction between basic and applied research is somewhat vague, I should like to adopt as the area in which the following suggestions are made the territory between the National Science Foundation's definition of industry basic research and the definition of applied research. The former indicates that basic research projects represent "original investigation for the advancement of scientific knowledge ... which do not have specific commercial objectives, although they may be in fields of present or potential interest to the reporting company." The latter indicates that applied research projects represent "investigations directed toward discovery of new scientific knowledge ... which have specific commercial objectives with respect to either products or processes."

1. Linkage between Flow-of-Funds Analysis and National Income Data

In the area of gross private domestic investing under the system of national accounts, capital flows and money markets have a great impact upon each of the various types of financial institutions and each of these in turn affect the market. Research completed on economic relationships in capital flow analysis is impressive, but it is just beginning to scratch the surface. The need for work in this area is great. In fact, many gaps still exist in the data and must be filled before full analysis can be made.

As an illustration, how life insurance company operations are treated in the consumer income, expenditure, and saving sectors within the system of national income accounts can be seen in Chart I, which shows present approximate distributions. The dual life insurance company function of insuring and investing requires special treatment in these accounts.

For example, the share of consumer spending on services that is accounted for by life insurance companies is measured in the national accounts by the amount spent for "handling" insurance. Actually this should hardly be called "handling"; it might better be termed "providing" life insurance through the efforts of a highly skilled staff of agents, investment analysts, actuaries, doctors, lawyers, and other personnel – supplemented by a complex of equipment and office space.

However, spending for providing life insurance is only part of premium and investment income, after the return flow of capital through payment of benefits to beneficiaries and living policyholders. Another part, the addition to reserves, surplus, and capital, is included in the savings sector of the national accounts.

These insurance funds also get into the GNP, but the route is far more complicated. For example, most funds show up in gross private domestic investing under plant and equipment expenditures and home building, but some show up in consumption expenditures because of loans made to installment credit companies, which help to finance the purchase of "big ticket" durable goods and services. Other funds show up in government

CHART I. Life Company Operations as Shown in the National Accounts

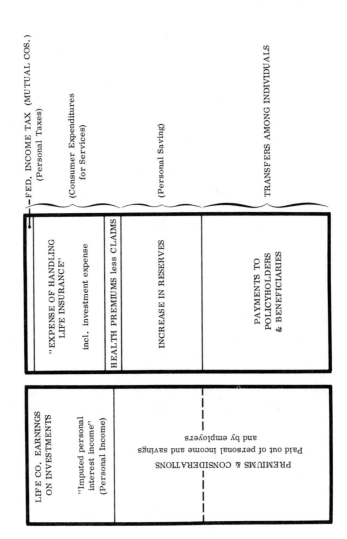

expenditures, both federal and local, for financing defense and nondefense projects. Still others show up in net foreign exports, in financing the production of products for sale abroad.

These lines of flow, though simple at first glance, are actually very complex. Research in economic thinking, utilizing data already available, might make the complex clearer and even simple.

Specifically, the formulation of the determinants of interest rates, both as to their levels and changes, is highly important to life insurance companies and other financial institutions. This involves the integration of all economic information shedding light on the supply and demand forces in the capital markets. It means that the spending decisions that comprise and create GNP must be related to the investment policies and practices of financial institutions, as well as to monetary and fiscal policies. When such relationships are established, the forecasting of changes in the various supply and demand factors should be feasible.

11. Better Utilization of Existing Facts for
Interindustry Analysis

In the area of fuller utilization of existing knowledge and data, new fields for research seem especially bright. Industries individually and collectively through trade associations have added importantly to the sum total of knowledge and are providing more and more data annually, quarterly, and monthly. Perhaps this can best be illustrated by the large number of fact books now available. Again, many of these are postwar products.

This list is not complete, but here are twenty-one books of facts regularly issued by industry and either directly involving financial institutions or indirectly relating to them.

Institute of Life Insurance. *Life Insurance Fact Book.*

Health Insurance Institute. *Source Book of Health Insurance Facts.*

Canadian Life Insurance Officers Assn. *Canadian Life Insurance Facts.*

Insurance Information Institute. *Property Insurance Fact Book.*

United States Savings and Loan League. *Savings and Loan Fact Book.*

National Association of Mutual Savings Banks. *Facts and Figures: Mutual Savings Banking.*

Investment Companies Institute. *Investment Companies Fact Book.*

New York Stock Exchange. *New York Stock Exchange Fact Book.*

Tax Foundation. *Fiscal Facts and Figures.*

American Gas Association. *Gas Facts.*

Edison Electric Institute. *Statistical Year Book of the Electric Utility Industry.*

Eastern Railroads Presidents Conference. *Yearbook of Railroad Information.*

National Association of Motor Bus Owners. *Bus Facts.*

Automobile Manufacturers Association. *Automobile Facts and Figures.*

Automobile Manufacturers Association. *Motor Truck Facts.*

Aerospace Industries Association of America. *Aerospace Facts and Figures*

Licensed Beverage Industries. *Alcoholic Beverage Industry Facts.*

Manufacturing Chemists' Association. *Chemical Industry Facts Book.*

Electronic Industries Association. *Electronics Industries Yearbook.*

National Paperboard Association. *Paperboard Industry Statistics.*

American Iron and Steel Institute. *Charting Steel's Progress: A Graphic Facts Book on the Iron and Steel Industry.*

Although these books are mainly composed of tabular materials, they also provide textual interpretation.

Obviously these basic fact books are being utilized. But there seems to be little doubt that they might be used even more intensively if they were related one to another. For example, what cause and effect comparisons might be determined in the financing relationship such as that between life insurance and steel, in the competitive relationship between savings and loan associations and investment companies, in the market relationship between property insurance and automobile facts and figures, in the developmental relationship between banks and the electronics industry, and so on?

III. Industry Performance and the Business Cycle

Although the life insurance business is not generally considered a cyclical industry, it nevertheless has felt the effects of the dozen or so business cycles in this century. Just briefly, good times produce a larger volume of policies issued, fewer controllable terminations, and increased premium income and annuity considerations. Bad times result in a smaller volume of policies issued, a greater demand for surrender values and policy loans, and an increased volume of lapsed policies.

Far more forward-looking research might be undertaken in the relationship of the performance of the several types of financial institutions in business cycle swings. This is especially important in the light of new thinking on postwar recession analysis, where only moderate downturns have taken place. As an illustration, in Chart II personal life insurance issued in the United States is compared with two recent cycles in industrial output. Each pair of curves indicates that, despite occasional irregular movements in insurance sales resulting from changes in the industry's operations, sales move in harmony with the economic climate of the country.

Moreover, the general mildness of postwar recessions might seem to indicate that when one is in the offing, nonacceptance of it by individuals and businesses might actually forestall its occurrence, or at least lessen its effects. In other words, if a recession seems to be coming, that may be exactly the time to increase and sharpen the efforts of individuals and businesses so that the effect of the recession can be lessened. This in effect

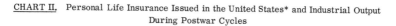

CHART II.   Personal Life Insurance Issued in the United States* and Industrial Output
During Postwar Cycles

(Seasonal eliminated; plotted monthly as a percentage of averages during each period)

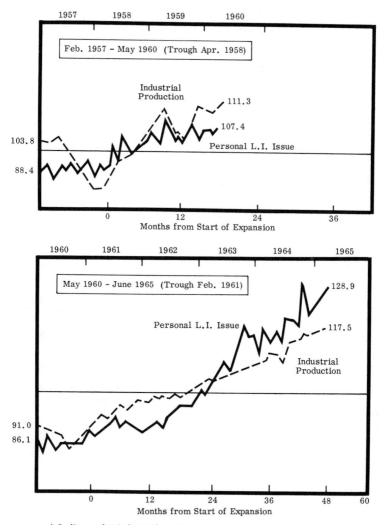

* Ordinary plus industrial, excluding wholesale and credit insurance.

(Note: These charts reflect different base years.)

means compensatory action from private sources, rather than dependence upon the government.

More specifically, this leads to a very interesting analogy concerning life insurance companies. It runs something like this:

1. Recessions are generally evidenced by a backup of inventories.

2. The inventory sector of gross private domestic investment includes no service industries, except for some supplies on hand.

3. The life insurance business, as a service industry, has no inventory problem.

4. Services are becoming a more important part of economic activity.

5. Therefore service industries, including life insurance companies, may help to moderate recessions by pushing sales.

IV. Regional and City Analysis

Since basic research in the area of economics and finance often is limited to national analyses, these might well be supplemented with investigation on a regional or city basis – but with the national objective in mind. True, a great deal of research is undertaken for marketing purposes by particular areas in cities. In many cases, however, there are only a few common denominators, like employment and perhaps income, that are available for interarea comparison and for composite compilation.

To be specific: When the nation's economy is evaluated for past, present, and future trends, sector analysis is perhaps the most popular means for setting up a forecast – whether by judgment model or by computer technique. Attempting to build a national total by adding up important city, suburban, and farm regions might provide some interesting checks and balances.

V. International Finance

Although United States life insurance companies neither sell their products abroad nor directly invest abroad, except in Canada, to any great extent, nevertheless events in the foreign sector of the economy are important to the industry. The inflationary aspects of the balance of payments deficit are especially significant. Moreover, life insurance companies have a very important stake in the well-being of United States corporations, which borrow funds for investment not only domestically but also abroad. Just how much of these life company funds indirectly flows abroad is not known.

Similarly, group policyholders engaged in foreign export and import competition form a direct tie between United States life insurance companies and international markets – as do individual policyholders who are employed by such firms.

A specific example for research is: What is the possible economic impact of the Common Market? Although the population of the present members of the Common Market almost equals the United States population of about 190 million, the anticipated expansion in the Common Market could raise its total to about 340 million people, or four-fifths again as large as that of the United States. This area could provide tough competition.

Although insurance is not a type of economic activity with which the Treaty of Rome, the basis of the Common Market, is primarily concerned, it and other financial services are specifically mentioned in Article 61, which states, "The liberalization of banking and insurance services connected with the movements of capital shall be effected in harmony with the progressive liberalization of the movement of capital." What are the problems that must be overcome before harmonization and nondiscrimination are realized? Obviously, they are not all going to be overcome, or even recognized, with the same ease with which this question is asked.

There are also many favorable factors. Insurance *can* be offered in far larger amounts than that for which there is presently a demand. It is obvious that the people of many countries are underinsured, and that in many instances it is impossible for any significant additional part of their present incomes to be allocated to premium payments after the barest essentials for living have been satisfied. However, with the expected expansion of economic activity through the Common Market, new doors may open for greater insurance coverage.

VI. *Improved Financial Data for Industry*

An area of basic economic research that would be especially useful for financial analysts might be the development of more detailed and prompt financial data for individual industries that would be useful as a yardstick for measuring the performance of a single company. Such data might also prove useful in better gauging the relative effects of cyclical fluctuations upon the financial position and flows of individual industries.

Balance sheet and operating data for the trade and service industries tend to be inadequate, dated, and frequently not available. It seems reasonable that the use of electronic data processing and the development of representative samples should permit prompt and reasonably accurate reporting of aggregate financial data by industry without violating the confidence of the individual reporting companies.

Areas of Finance Requiring Further Basic Research

Robert F. Vandell
Professor of Business Administration
Graduate School of Business Administration
University of Virginia

THE question before me is: What areas of the financial world do I personally think warrant additional basic research at this time? My answers reflect my interest as an academician, albeit a pragmatically oriented one, in learning how financial officers of firms can make better decisions in areas of importance to their firms.

An impressive amount of financial research is going on at the moment. Much of it is being done by practicing financial officers and is pointed toward providing the data required to make some immediate decisions. Other individuals are searching simply for an understanding of basic financial relationships that may remain too abstract to have any practical value for many years to come. Still other researchers follow programs that have objectives reflecting varying blends of the abstract theoretical and the concrete practical.

My first interest is in seeing that we make the most of research currently in progress. At the practical end of the spectrum, the record is not good. Although financial officers exchange ideas and endeavor through training to pass their craftsmanship on to their successors, the process is probably not very efficient. When a particular businessman faces a decision, it may be very difficult for him to tap the wisdom of those individuals who have already spent considerable time analyzing and resolving closely similar issues. Moreover, the wisdom born of the experience of the most thoughtful and perceptive financial executives seldom gets recorded and accumulated in a manner that can be passed down systematically and widely to the new generation of executive talent. In short, we need more effective ways of gathering and pooling the research findings already available.

It is also imperative for practitioners to recognize how the revolution in information technology can affect decision making in their firms. It is now possible for decision makers to demand more information preprocessed more systematically but at a lower cost per item to help evaluate the action alternatives confronting them. Financial officers, facing issues that tend to be more amenable to extensive quantitative analysis, should be among the vanguard of those striving to find more systematic and thorough analytical techniques. While considerable skepticism about the ultimate contributions of the new management science is appropriate, an opportunity and a need to press toward the limits at a faster pace do exist. No doubt researchers outside as well as in firms can still find many ways of developing or adapting generally useful approaches to information processing that will contribute toward this progress.

Of more immediate pertinence is the need for greater knowledge of what is really going on in the financial world. I refer to knowledge that lies beyond the feasible range of analysis of the financial officer faced with a stream of urgent problems.

In its most abstract form, the principal economic task of management is to maximize the welfare of the firm's owners, usually by maximizing the present worth of the stock. How is this to be done? Theories constructed to date are very limited inasmuch as they incorporate at least the first three and usually more of the following assumptions, which are presented overly cryptically: (a) capital markets are purely competitive, (b) each investor is motivated solely by prospects of economic gain and can move freely to whatever investment will optimize his return, (c) the market is in continuous equilibrium so that individual prices are related to an adjudgment of the present worth of the firm's dividend stream from that moment to infinity, (d) there is no uncertainty, (e) there are no transfer costs in buying or selling stocks or in issuing new securities, and (f) corporate or personal taxes do not influence decisions of corporate officers or investors.[1] All these hypotheses require some qualification, and some appear to be completely false. Until we can develop and integrate more realistic hypotheses, theoretical conclusions may be quite misleading.

At the moment we know very little about how much of the volume of funds will be channeled into important segments of the capital markets, such as the common stock market, or how the funds will be distributed among the competing alternatives. This is because we do not know enough about how the various important investor types make the decisions that produce changes in demand patterns for and within a market, or how these decisions change with circumstances. Moreover, we do not know the circumstances causing supplies of securities to swell or fall. All of these forces influence values in ways material to officers shaping corporate financing and investment policies. But we don't know how.

There is also a need for more precise information about the character of the risks assumed when various types of senior financial securities are issued by a firm. Naturally, the magnitudes of uncertainties confronting a firm will make it impossible to determine in advance an exact measure of risk. Nevertheless, it should be feasible to determine what the consequences of these actions are going to be for the firm, its management, and its ownership. How can management better recognize the symptoms of serious financial adversity as early as possible – well before default – in order to take those actions that are most likely to reduce the seriousness of the risks ahead? We do not have very good evidence to answer these questions, and as a result analysis tends to be undesirably shallow too often. More research would certainly be welcomed here, and yet this is just an example of how understanding more about what is relevant to the decision makers in financial intermediaries can be useful to financial officers of corporations.

At a more general level, there is much we do not know about our capital markets that would help various decision makers,

---

[1] See further, John Lintner, "Dividends, Earnings, Leverage, Stock Prices and the Supply of Capital to Corporations," *Review of Economics and Statistics,* August 1962.

ranging from government regulators to investors, to complete better evaluations. Let me briefly tick off a few that I find matters of concern. In what ways do the present and potential capital market forces influence the achievement of national objectives? What are the effects throughout the capital markets system of governmental actions taken to regulate certain sectors? How quickly do changes in one sector of the market lead to marked changes in other sectors? Are we providing adequate incentives for risk taking in the market as a whole and, now that industrial firms are carrying on a larger portion of research, within corporations? What are rates of return in regulated or semiregulated industries sufficient to provide for satisfactory rates of investment, in view of the risks? In particular, I refer to recent pressures on pricing policies in the steel, mutual fund, and aluminum industries. What forces could cause a contraction in prices of securities sufficient to create psychological repercussions affecting economic activity levels materially? How does the desire for liquidity affect various important decision makers in the capital markets under various cyclical circumstances? Are the size and kinds of financial institutions servicing the capital markets ideal, or has government policy led to unwanted and disfunctional aberrations? Is the over-all quality of the portfolios of certain institutions improving or worsening, and, if the changes are for the worse, are they seriously so? Does the flow of savings through intermediaries rather than coming directly from individuals with differing interests and capacities for risk taking lead to a useful over-all distribution of investment funds in the various kinds of securities and security-risk classes? Has channeling "money" competition into service rather than price forms created the equivalent of administered prices? What cyclical threats, if any, exist because of the level and volatility of consumer demand for credit? And so on. It is hard not to think of an area where more research on the inter-relationships existing in the capital market would not be useful in helping to make important decisions.

Extract from Letter

Gilbert H. Palmer
Vice President The National City Bank of Cleveland

AS YOU may know from meetings of the CFA Trustees, I am a long-time advocate of research in the direction of the so-called "technical" approach to security analysis. Perhaps this would not qualify as basic research, but you will be the judge of that. While statistics of the market point to the increasing proportion of "professional" business, this has not inhibited the technicians. On the contrary, the "technical" approach seems to have gained in stature, acquiring more and more professional advocates, and it could be in a position to do real damage to the investing public and to financial markets.

It seems to me that this idea opens up a number of areas of research.

1. The "technical" approach needs a thoughtful and thorough definition related to its *purposes* among other things.

2. A survey is needed to explore – I was about to say "explode the myth of " – its value as an analytical method. There have been some antitechnical studies, none very compelling, but to my knowledge not a single serious work defending the method. Perhaps this is one of the problems. The technicians are like the saxophone player who didn't have to *prove* he was the best in the world; he *admitted* it. How can you refute that?

3. Does the point-and-figure method, as an example, have enough advocates to affect markets materially? Do interpretations of various practitioners coincide?

4. Can we measure the impact of technical advice (services, market letters, and the like) on market volume? This would include "professional" volume as well as the individual trader.

5. How widespread is the acceptance of technical analysis among analysts and security salesmen?

6. Assuming *some* degree of damaging evidence can be produced, what can be done about it?

Number 6 is a major area for "speculative thinking," as it was put in the letter. The financial woods are full of technicians. Their life is such an easy one that their numbers seem likely to grow vigorously. Opposition to the trend has become downright unpopular, and a lot of education is sorely needed.

Extract from Letter

Jonathan A. Brown
Director of Research
New York Stock Exchange

ABOUT three years ago I was asked to serve on a committee established by the NBER to identify topics similar to those mentioned in Dean Abbott's letter deserving attention in the next few years. The committee's report, *Research in the Capital Markets,** was published as a supplement to the May 1964 issue of the *Journal of Finance*. In large part, I would suppose that the committee's findings are still valid, though I did not concur in all the recommendations. Your current survey, however, may well point out additional areas where research would appear fruitful. It may also aid in establishing priorities and stimulating specific action.

A considerable amount of research is, of course, now under way. In addition to several projects at the NBER, work directly related to securities is in progress at the University of Chicago and at the University of Pennsylvania's Wharton School, to name two organizations with whose work I am somewhat familiar. Also, it can be hoped that the study papers developed for the Commission on Money and Credit will generate further research by the authors and others over a period of time.

Nevertheless, there is always more to be done. As the chairman pointed out in his preface to the NBER report, "The wide range of subjects makes it evident that no single individual, group of individuals, or research organization could hope to undertake more than a fraction of the whole." Although I have not taken the opportunity to review the status of current projects in detail, I have jotted down in the following paragraphs a few of the problems that appear to me to be especially significant for further work.

---

*For a condensation of this, see Appendix B.

First of all, it seems to me that we need to know a great deal more about the role of the money supply in our economy. A fundamental problem is whether causality runs from the money supply to the level of activity in the economy, from the economy to the money supply, or in both directions, depending on circumstances. The effect on the securities markets, both bonds and equities, would be especially interesting. Certain views on this subject raise critical and provocative questions for our future monetary policy. Much work remains to be done, however, to establish the degree of causality, if any, as an aid to future monetary action.

A somewhat related problem, which should and will attract much attention in the next few years, is the effect on fiscal lag of seasonality in the federal cash budget. Individual social security tax payments, for example, as well as April 15 personal income tax payments, tend to be concentrated in the first half of the year, with notable seasonal influences on federal cash needs. Measurement of the seasonal impact and ways of alleviating this phenomenon could lead to useful policy recommendations.

Another area where I feel that research is needed is in evaluating the many factors which affect the supply and demand of services offered by various types of institutions to the public. One question in this area is the impact of the distribution of the public's demand for financial institutional services on the distribution of various forms of financing within the economy. For example, a substantial public demand for life insurance or for savings and loan shares will result in relatively less money available for equity investment. This is because the contractual, legal, and other obligations of these types of institutions require them to keep a relatively high proportion of their assets in nonequity investments. Thus, the nature of the public's demand for various institutional services determines, in part, the allocation of funds flowing into the capital markets.

Of probably equal importance is the demand side of the capital markets. What relative weight should be given to the various factors that affect business decisions as to the form of external financing employed? In terms of the long-run growth of the firm rather than the short-run effect on profits, is debt financing preferable to equity? Put another way, what is the optimum debt-equity ratio for companies in various industries? Is our economy feeding on too much debt? If so, where and why, and what can we do about it?

I would suggest that there is an opportunity for much worthwhile analysis in the changing relationships between various types of financial institutions and their customers. The NBER's report, for example, contains an extensive discussion of needed studies of the flow of funds into and out of securities. The changing patterns of financial asset ownership offer fertile ground for detailed analysis, but efforts to date in this field have really only scratched the surface. Serious attention should be given to the problem of whether current tax policy unduly encourages institutional and contractual savings.

I hope that some of the foregoing suggestions are in line with the general concept of "basic research" studies which you believe might be profitably undertaken if adequate financial and manpower resources were made available. Intentionally omitted are some of the major research problems of the day, such as taxes, the balance of payments, and international monetary reform, as they do not seem to be within your scope.

PART IV

Financial Markets and Governmental Influence

Commentary

THE financial business is the most heavily regulated of all industries. It is also more closely related to and more intimately affected by federal fiscal affairs, monetary policy, and Treasury operations than any other area of business activity.

Generally speaking, governmental influence and regulation in the financial world are directed toward three objectives: economic stability at a high level of employment, support of the Treasury in its financial operations, and control of practices by private financial institutions that, at one time or another, have been deemed abuses.

Two related questions regarding governmental influence are continually raised, implicitly or explicitly, throughout this collection, as well as in the papers grouped in Part IV: Does the totality of governmental rules and regulations stemming from the numerous regulatory bodies constitute a logically consistent whole? Is the regulatory framework *in fact* well designed to accomplish its stated purposes and at the same time encourage economic growth? Douglas A. Hayes suggests: "It would seem that basic research into the theory and practice of governmental regulation of financial functions would be a highly appropriate area of investigation." Careful reading of this collection suggests that the significant observation to be made concerning governmental influence in the financial world may be that *if* there is a systematic, logically consistent scheme underlying the government's posture the contributors to this symposium seem unaware of it.

The memoranda placed in this section do not, for the most part, take a broad overview of the subject. Rather they stress particular facets and consequences of governmental influence and, implicitly, raise the question whether an extended sense of responsibility on the part of the private sector of the economy is likely to produce a society that is more satisfactory to live in than would be produced by an extended sense of responsibility in the public sector.

The points emphasized in the contributions to this symposium set some of the parameters of the subject, though they are far from constituting a comprehensive enumeration. Ralph F. Leach concentrates on the role and functioning of the government securities market. Since this market is at the heart of all securities markets and, indeed, of the entire financial process, it seems impossible to overemphasize the importance to the whole economy of its health, freedom, and breadth. George E. Shea, Jr., like Jonathan A. Brown in Part III, queries whether credit and finance influence business activity, or merely reflect it. This uncertainty clearly is a crucial one, both in monetary theory and in the operation of fiscal policy – particularly if fiscal policy, implemented through Treasury operations and manipulation of the market for Treasury obligations, is viewed as the principal mechanism for affecting the level of business activity. Joseph A. Livingston raises a series of questions regarding the roles and relations of the private and the public sectors of the financial world – questions that clearly impinge on the memoranda of Ralph F. Leach and George E. Shea. Similarly Beryl W. Sprinkel, utilizing both economic theory and economic history, suggests that we may not know as much as we like to think we do about either the past or present relationships of private financial institutions and public bodies. And Douglas A. Hayes, while surveying a host of considerations that bear on this range of problems, very properly introduces the importance of qualitative, subjective judgments and ethical standards. As he properly points out, if the private components of the economy take the position that "long-run problems of the domestic economic and social environment ... are outside the scope of their concern ... , then public demands for solution will lead to action by the public sector." In that event dialogues regarding the appropriate roles of private and public institutions do indeed become exercises in futility.

Extract from Letter

Ralph F. Leach
Executive Vice President and Treasurer
Morgan Guaranty Trust Company of New York

AS FAR as new basic research is concerned, my suggestions relate primarily to the government securities market, with particular reference to the viability of that market under the changed ground rules since 1961.

One of the suggestions that we have made which could be said to be in the area of basic research is a switch to a monthly staggered reserve settlement plan for Federal Reserve member banks. An article on this subject was published in the *Journal of Finance* in March 1964, and a follow-up commentary was published in the same *Journal* in September 1964. We would like to see some outside unit study this suggestion critically, with the hope that it would either be dismissed due to lack of feasibility or, hopefully, if endorsed, adopted by the Federal Reserve. It is our contention that the present system is anachronistic and that greater reliance on a market mechanism could obviate as much as 75 percent of the present volume of open market operations by the Federal Reserve.

Another area of fruitful investigation would be that of the composition of the Federal Reserve's holdings of United States Treasury securities. A study in this area could run the gamut from the question of the type of securities and optimum maturity distributions all the way to the Patman question of cancellation of some portion of the portfolio. The Patman proposal is much more difficult to dispose of logically than most students in this area seem to think.

We would also like to see some thought given to the problem of Treasury trust accounts and their investment activities. A good case could probably be made for using only special issues of a nonmarketable nature for most or all of such accounts. This, of course, would obviate the problem of debt managers changing hats periodically and becoming investment advisers in the securities whose issuance they govern.

Ultimately all of these suggestions relate to the freedom of the market for government securities and the ability of the monetary authorities to obtain a meaningful signal from the fixed income markets. It has long been our feeling that the movement of interest rates can hardly be meaningful to authorities whose constant preoccupation is with the management of the interest rate structure.

The same type of question can be raised about international exchange markets. With the entry of the Federal Reserve into day-to-day activities involving the major international currencies we have certainly reached the point where fluctuations in prices of these currencies cannot be used as reliable indicators either by the market place or by the authorities. In this area we have probably gone a step further so that even the official statistics which are being released are doctored to the point of unreliability.

Challenges to the Financial Community

Douglas A. Hayes
Professor of Finance
Graduate School of Business Administration
The University of Michigan

IN VERY broad terms the role of the finance community in the economy can be visualized as the process of mobilizing the resources of "surplus units" (those units with a flow of income or other receipts in excess of current outlays) and making them available to "deficit units" (those units with expenditure programs in excess of current income flows). Of course it should be noted that the availability of resources to "deficit units" may be greater than the supply generated from "surplus units" to the extent that there is a net expansion of bank earning assets and deposits.

As corollaries to the basic function of financial process, the institutional structure directs its energies to providing incentives for "surplus units" both to maximize the amounts of their savings and to commit them either directly or through financial intermediaries to the financing of "deficit units." The creative development of attractive financial instruments and the provision of reasonable liquidity thereon, i.e., secondary markets, can be considered to be the major means of implementing this objective.

In a very basic sense the research issues that emerge are whether the existing institutional structure performs the several functions outlined above in a manner that provides adequate service and responsibility to its clients, "surplus" and "deficit" units, on the one hand and to society at large on the other. Comprehensive objective research on these matters is very difficult for several reasons.

First, subjective value judgments are necessarily involved. For example, it can be argued that these functions should be evaluated in terms of their effects on the quality of human activity and environment as well as in terms of their effects on the quantity of goods and service generated through time. Differences in value judgments along these lines seem to be inherent in much of the controversy as to the appropriate allocation of resources as between the public and private sectors and to the desirable degree of regulation of the latter sector. In my opinion, research on the financial functions should incorporate qualitative values as well as quantitative values into its conclusions and recommendations. Otherwise, almost by definition, the conclusions can be held inapplicable to desirable policy decisions within either the public or private sector.

Second, in our complex society the institutional structure has become highly fragmented and diverse. It is true, of course, that a major research objective might be to inquire critically into whether the existing institutional structure does in fact contribute or detract from the optimal performance of the several finance functions. But because the structure includes commercial banks, investment banks, insurance companies, and savings institutions, as well as ordinary corporations and individuals, such a project would be of enormous dimensions.

Third, governmental regulatory intrusion into the financial functions is considerably more detailed and extensive with respect to both statutory and administrative law than in other functional areas of economic activity such as production and distribution. The intrusions have been justified generally on one or more of the following grounds: (a) the need to protect the public against manipulation and fraud – the Securities and Exchange Act; (b) the special fiduciary position of many financial institutions – insurance and banking regulations; (c) the singular role of the commercial banks in creating and extinguishing the money supply – Federal Researve monetary controls; (d) the desire to prevent undue concentrations of economic power – branch banking limitations.

It would seem that basic research into the theory and practice of governmental regulation of financial functions would be a highly appropriate area of investigation. It would consider the effects of regulation on the optimal allocation of economic resources and power, economic growth, and the strength of the financial system as compared to what they might be if the principles of competitive free enterprise were substituted for much of the regulatory framework. Again, however, it would be difficult to avoid undue immersion in the great detail of regulatory practices in order to concentrate on the broad economic and social consequences of governmental prescriptions.

A related inquiry might be concerned with the subject of ethical standards and their enforcement in the performance of the finance functions. Unfortunately there is no financial "profession" as such which can be made subject to rules of entry and punishment by exclusion as is true for the legal and medical professions. The crucial issue is whether ethical standards of a meaningful sort can be established, and more importantly enforced, to guide the diverse activities in the financial structure. Possibly the hypothesis of the need for compulsory ethical standards might be questioned on the ground that the doctrine of caveat emptor should apply. But it has become increasingly clear that public policy will not tolerate the consequences of the latter doctrine. Therefore, unless the financial community can prove a consistent and complete adherence to high standards of conduct in its relations with the public at large, it will inevitably be both suspect and subject to considerable control to protect the public interest.

The communication inviting this memorandum made reference to "speculative thinking" with respect to the services rendered by the financial community. This observation can be interpreted to mean comments both on the nature of such services and the methods of achieving compensation for their performance. As purely a "speculative" thought, the idea may be advanced that the traditional method of compensation for services rendered customers in the secondary markets may inherently tend to induce substandard conduct to some extent. In these markets compensation is based on the volume of transactions generated in customer accounts. The consequences may be inclinations (a) to recommend excessive "turnovers" of clients' holdings and (b) to induce the preparation of a steady stream of trading advice related both to individual securities and the market as a whole. In my opinion, this material on balance greatly reinforces the popular image of the securities markets as essentially quasi-gambling casinos.

The purpose of these observations is merely to raise the questions: (a) whether transactions should determine compensation in the secondary markets, and (b) whether any possible alternatives would be equitable and practicable. One hypothesis for any research in this connection would seem to be that the methods of compensation should be established so as to produce ethical behavior of the highest sort. Research along these lines might also be directed to the appropriate institutional framework for other types of financial services where a professional-client relationship is indicated to a considerable extent.

Finally, it is becoming increasingly clear that effective checks on the expansion of the public sector cannot be expected unless the various components of the private sector, including the financial community, can identify in a positive way with some important long-run problems of the domestic economic and social environment. If these components take the position that these problems are outside the scope of their concern or merely ignore them, then public demands for solution will lead to action by the public sector. For example, the problems of water and air pollution and land despoilment are becoming increasingly critical as ancillary consequences of population and industrial growth. The long-run survival of a congenial physical environment probably depends upon their solution, but to date the private sector has largely maintained a negative posture on these problems unless prodded by public agencies.

Unless some means can be found to incorporate positive and effective action on these matters within the private sector, demands for retrenchment of public sector programs will become increasingly irrelevant and obviously absurd. In my opinion, the most important long-term issue faced by the private sector, including finance, is how its services can be adapted to meet these crucial problems because unless the problems can be met, a continued erosion of the role of the private sector appears inevitable.

Extract from Letter

George E. Shea, Jr.
Financial Editor
The Wall Street Journal

DO CREDIT and finance really.have much influence on business, or do they merely reflect it? My own feeling is that the power of finance to control economic events or even to influence them much is greatly overestimated. I have two examples in mind. One is the postwar boom in Germany in spite of relative shortages of capital and high interest rates compared with conditions here. My impression from this experience is that if business is on the way up it will find ways to finance itself regardless of the obstacles.

The other example is the fact that in the 1929–32 depression bank deposits, both demand and time, rose the first year. That is, from the end of 1929 to the end of 1930 deposits rose even though business, production, and goods prices were falling. Then, in 1931, 1932, and 1933, deposits joined the downtrend. This fact suggests to me that business didn't turn down because of financial difficulties in the aggregate, even though there were numerous bank and other failures, but that the downturn in business itself was the prime mover. Of course, this gets into business-cycle theory, which can fill and has filled whole tomes.

The other thought has to do with the seeming tendency to make changes in the structure of the financial system to enable it more and more to escape control by the FRB. I refer, for instance, to the fact that nonbank institutions have grown much faster than the banking system. I also refer to the new ways banks have found of enhancing their capital for lending and investing, such as the issuance of certificates of deposit, which require relatively small reserves, and the issuance of capital notes, which require none.

Extract from Letter

Beryl W. Sprinkel
Vice President and Economist
Harris Trust and Savings Bank

ONE important and interesting development that has occurred in the financial markets in the past few years is the increased role of commercial banking in the intermediation process. Commercial banks to an increasing extent have accepted short-term deposits in varying forms and have used such funds to make longer-term loans and investments. Several questions arise with respect to this development. Is the trend recently observable a new one or is it merely an acceleration of a long-observable pattern? What factors were responsible for the recent changes? Were the factors changes in regulatory patterns or changes in the attitude of bank management, as some people suggest? What questions develop with respect to implications concerning the soundness of the banking industry and also with respect to stability of the economy? Is this tendency likely to continue and, if so, what does this pattern suggest for the probable developments in competitive industries?

In recent years there seems to be an increasing concern about possible unsustainability of the rapid expansion in private debt. Frequently the analysis avoids discussion of reasonable alternatives to private debt expansion. Throughout the discussion of a possible change in our tax structure, very little attention was devoted to the possibility of eliminating or reducing the current bias against equity investment. Would the stability of our economy be improved if a larger percentage of new financing were achieved through the equity route instead of through debt? If so, what tax changes should be developed to bring this about?

Many of the regulations of financial institutions including banks were developed as an aftermath of the Great Depression.

The prevailing view appeared to be that private excesses, particularly in the financial sphere, were responsible for the size and longevity of the Great Depression. This view has come under severe attack as a result of recent research by such people as Milton Friedman and Anna Schwartz. The new view appears to hold that the excesses during this period were primarily governmental and not private, and, in particular, much of the responsibility is placed upon the FRS, which did not respond in an expansive way once the decline began. If the latter view is correct, this would suggest that a reappraisal of the resulting financial regulations is long past due. In fact, under the sponsorship of James J. Saxon, Comptroller of the Currency, many of the regulatory restrictions upon banking have been relaxed. It is conceivable that many of the financial regulations have severely reduced the ability of financial institutions to meet the needs of a growing and changing economy. A study reviewing the nature of the financial regulations, the probable impact upon financial practices, and an evaluation of the desirability of reducing or changing these restrictions might well yield substantial long-run benefits to the economy.

In recent years there seems to be increasing concern about the possible deterioration in the "quality of credit." Implicit in this view is the belief that the market place, representing the interaction of borrowers and lenders, is no longer capable of rendering sound credit judgments. If this view were to gather increased support, it might well lead to further regulation of the credit mechanism. It is admittedly difficult to measure the extent to which the quality of credit has deteriorated, and, so far as I know, the question has never been asked whether deterioration in credit quality is always an unmitigated evil. A research project designed to investigate the efficacy of the market process in this area might well be worth while.

Basic Research on the Role of the Financial Community in the Economy

Joseph A. Livingston
Financial Editor
Philadelphia Bulletin

FIRST, let me question an assumption. The letter suggests that research should examine "what the behavior and characteristics of financial institutions and the private financial world should be if they are to act as an effective check on the expansion of the public sector." Certainly the private sector is important to financing, but so is the public sector. Therefore, I respectfully suggest that basic research should not start with an a priori conclusion. How do we know that expansion of the public sector should be checked? Maybe it ought to be expanded or stay just where it is.

I bring this up because I have wondered for a long time whether the vast effort that goes into the distribution of private capital is justified. I refer specifically to the elaborate Wall Street apparatus – the daily trading on the New York Stock Exchange in stocks and bonds – requiring thousands of brokerage firms and many more thosands of floor brokers and telephone traders.

The mere question challenges assumptions we have all been brought up on – the liquidity of the market place. Let me throw out one question: Would the market be any less liquid if only one trade took place in a stock in a day? Banks could base loans on securities on prices set once a day. And think how much man effort would be eliminated. Mutual funds establish selling and buying prices once or twice a day. Why could not a once-a-day auction system be used to set the price of U.S. Steel or AT & T?

It is true that we in the United States have the finest capital market of any nation in the world, with the possible exception of

Great Britain. We assume that our system selects, through the interplay of market forces, those industries most deserving of capital. We assume that our Wall Street system of distribution is responsible for the excellence – the breadth and depth – of our capital market.

But it would be well to establish this by basic research. Our system offers seekers of capital multiple opportunities to go to Lehman Brothers, Drexel & Company, Morgan Stanley, and so on for funds. A rejection by one is not total as in the Soviet Union and other totalitarian economies, where the planners meet and decide which enterprises get funds. The horizons of the men in the Kremlin and those who report to them limit the decisions. But let us not forget that this system produced the first Sputnik and the first man in space. And it could be – I throw this out for analysis – that the wealth of our country is responsible for the capital markets. Is the throwoff of savings so great that any capital-savings method would work?

The private capital market has its limitations, too. It directs capital into activities which have profit-bearing potentialities. Socially desirable projects such as pure research, disassociated from profit – Sputnik, for instance – are outside the private capital market. And if a project is extremely large and vested with public interest – Comsat, for example – the government gets involved. No private company can undertake the building of prototype supersonic planes without government help. Thus, size – the great cost – of modern technology may have rendered obsolete our system of providing capital to enterprise.

Therefore, I suggest a thorough examination of all of our postulates about Wall Street. How important is liquidity? How important is competition in the sale of securities? Is it necessary to have thousands of salesman selling stocks and bonds or selling mutual funds? Society, as the employer and beneficiary of capital, must pay for the effort that goes into channeling the community's savings to IBM or Comsat, or Wellington Fund, and the cats and dogs – companies that never get anywhere.

The study should also examine the validity of the theory that young, struggling companies get their start through finding capital in the market place. The efforts of the government to provide funds through the SBA and SBIC's suggest that these needs have not been entirely met by the private sector. Maybe they never can be. This, in itself, warrants a presumption contrary to that in the first paragraph of the letter about checking expansion of the public sector.

I realize that I have taken off on an unorthodox tangent. But basic research can only get somewhere if orthodoxy is reexamined, if built-in convictions are analyzed, if the institutions by which men swear are demonstrated to be useful, efficient, and necessary.

PART V

Intermediaries: Problems of Communication, Conflicts of Interest, Economic Analysis

Commentary

DURING the last fifteen years or more the growth of financial intermediaries, of institutionally held shares, of the "pool of managed money," of the "paraproprietal society," has been enormous. The prospect is for further growth, perhaps on an even larger scale.

A priori reasoning, even without examination of the facts, would suggest that this development has been accompanied by a variety of problems, challenges, and opportunities for businessmen and economists alike. Study of the memoranda in this collection, both those in this and in other sections, substantiates this conclusion. Careful reading of the symposium suggests two main areas of concern, each with a number of subdivisions.

The first of these may be loosely categorized as containing business problems that in large measure grow out of difficulties of communication occasioned by changes in structure and in relationships within the financial world. Here we find questions of communication among beneficial owners, professional management, and financial intermediaries; questions concerning the responsibilities of men who manage other peoples' money in the "pool of managed money"; possible conflicts of interest; concern regarding the socialization of wealth in the investment companies; insufficient public understanding of the new institutional structure and its significance; in some instances a lack of public confidence in the financial world. The contributions, among others, of Howard C. Tharsing, Ora C. Roehl, Robert C. Kirby, Albert Y. Bingham and Everett G. Judson all touch, in different ways, on this range of subject matter. Three questions, out of many that could be cited, will be illustrative:

> If the financial intermediaries are to continue to grow both absolutely and relatively as efficient conduits between the saver and the capital demands of

the national economy, then increased responsibility must sooner or later be accepted. – Robert C. Kirby

The question of the relationship of the financial community with business owners seems to me to be worth considerable research effort.... Perhaps the basic subject ... is: Are financial institutions chiefly a conduit for funds – with very limited responsibilities – or should they act as "trustees" for the principals? – Howard C. Tharsing

It has long been a source of concern that commercial banks are given access to almost all figures, budgets, and other data helpful to the management ... whereas most vehicles such as mutual funds and others who handle other people's money are often allowed no information except what is released to all stockholders. – Albert Y. Bingham

The "technical" approach [to stock market analysis] needs a thoughtful and thorough definition related to its *purposes*....

Does the point-and-figure method, as an example, have enough advocates to affect markets materially? Do interpretations of various practitioners coincide? – Gilbert H. Palmer

We do not know enough about how the various important investor types make the decisions that produce changes in demand patterns for and within a market, nor how these decisions change with circumstances. Moreover, we do not know the circumstances causing supplies of securities to swell or fall. – Robert F. Vandell

Does increased efficiency in business result in more goods and services produced per dollar of asset investment?

Or is greater automation leading to greater asset investment per dollar of output?

Is there a trend in demand for goods and services ... requiring comparatively smaller asset investment? – Bion G. Howard

One question ... is the impact of the distribution of the public's demand for financial institutional services on the distribution of various forms of financing within the economy. – Jonathan A. Brown.

In the light of these comments, who is bold enough to say that we can define the critical factors that determine the behavior of capital markets or that we could assess their performance if measured by yardsticks that we wish we had?

Long-Range Social, Economic, and Political Responsibilities of the Financial Intermediaries

Robert G. Kirby
Assistant to the President
Capital Research and Management Company

ONE worthy project might be a study of the long-range social, economic, and political responsibilities of the managers of investment companies, pension trusts, profit-sharing trusts, and similar pools of investment capital. These institutions have grown at an incredible pace in terms of capital under supervision during the past fifteen years. The movement of capital from the investor or saver into business investment in the form of plant and equipment has changed drastically in recent decades, just as control of capital and control of the means of production have shifted from a relatively few daring entrepreneurs to a much-broader-based segment of the population acting on a more objective and scientific basis.

The financial intermediaries have been a product of and have helped to facilitate this change. If their growth over the next two decades is anywhere near an extension of the past decade or two, they may have to consider accepting responsibilities far beyond their present scope of activity.

Today's society includes strong population segments that literally did not exist fifty or one hundred years ago. Perhaps the most powerful such segment is the professional business management group. This group is highly trained, affluent, and young; it constitutes only a minor ownership position in the businesses that it manages. Another segment might be called working capitalists. This group of relatively small investors is rapidly growing in number and has increasingly placed its investment decisions in the hands of professionally trained financial intermediaries such as the managers of pension and profit-sharing trusts and the managers of investment companies.

The net result of these trends is certainly that today's decisions in the fields of business and investment tend to be made more objectively and more scientifically, based on more complete and adequate data, but there is a growing breakdown of communication between the owners and the managers of "big business." The professional business manager has different motivation and feels different responsibilities than his counterpart at the beginning of the century. He recognizes an obligation to government (local and national), to his employees, and to his customers that is not appreciably less than his obligation to the owners of the business. Further, of these groups whose diverse, and sometimes conflicting, interests he is attempting to serve, the shareowners are the segment that seems to have the least ability to make its wishes known or to influence management.

Inevitably, more of the burden of acting as appraiser, critic, and watchdog of the management performance of publicly owned companies falls onto the shoulders of the financial intermediaries. These intermediaries, however, whether insurance companies, trust companies, or investment companies, almost universally as a matter of policy decline to take any action that would directly influence the management of the businesses in which they have investments. In an environment where 20 or 25 percent, or more, of many substantial companies is owned by financial institutions, and where, in most cases, this percentage is growing, the institutions' posture as passive shareholders is subject to challenge.

The transition of the past fifty years or so from entrepreneur managements to nonowner professional managements in publicly owned companies has seen very little decline in the ability of management to be self-perpetuating. The common stocks of a good many companies listed on the New York Stock Exchange could really be called nonvoting in a *de facto* sense. If the shares are held by an individual investor who disapproves of the performance of management, it is a virtually impossible task for him to organize sufficient support to exert any influence. If the stock is owned by a financial institution that disapproves of the performance of management, that institution simply sells its holding as the only necessary corrective measure.

If the financial intermediaries are to continue to grow both absolutely and relatively as efficient conduits between the saver and the capital demands of the national economy, then increased responsibility must sooner or later be accepted. As time passes, the publicly held corporations are likely to continue to grow, corporate managements and individual shareowners are likely to have less and less of an ownership position, and individual shareowners are likely to have less and less ability to make their desires known to management. To date the financial intermediary has accepted only the research responsibility, the responsibility to appraise and to select rather than to criticize. It is very difficult to see how the existing pattern can be continued unchanged. A much broader responsibility exists somewhere in this complex that no one has yet been willing to accept. The magnitude of this responsibility seems likely to grow substantially with the passage of time. It seems clear that a major factor accounting for the reluctance of financial intermediaries to depart from their traditional roles as passive investors is fear of greater control and influence by the federal government. However, it is also possible that the absence of effective lines of communication between typical shareholders represented by the financial intermediaries and the businesses in which their capital is invested will result in greater federal control through the assumption of this responsibility by government.

Basic Research in the Financial World

Everett G. Judson
Vice President and Director
Keystone Custodian Funds, Inc.

CONCERN that not enough basic research is being conducted in the private financial world appears well founded. The ABA, the NASD, the ICI – the principal agencies representative of the private effort – are far overshadowed in this respect by the FRB and the SEC. As a result of its basic research into the banking system and its powers over bank trust and savings departments, the FRB exerts great influence in the affairs of the private financial world. The SEC has repeatedly conducted basic research, but all too frequently the private financial world has not been in a situation to respond effectively to the findings.

Most important to the long-run interests of all private financial institutions is understanding of the functions of such institutions in our free enterprise system. Initially, a research effort designed to develop a nationwide educational program, within the private financial community, is called for in order that all interests directly concerned may understand the wisdom and desirability of conducting a coordinated effort. Such a program should be designed to serve the interests of all those institutions active in the field of private finance, not any particular special interests. Unless those directly involved believe that what is good for the community serves the best interests of the various elements, then any attempt to enlighten the public generally will fall far short of success.

Further, an all-important private goal is to educate the public in the theory of profit – that profit is not simply a residual income factor but rather *the* vital element of the nation's savings, and therefore the key to our free enterprise system. The future of the financial community, just as that of every manufacturing company, rests on the profit motive. Without the services provided

by financial institutions, our entire economic process would
hurriedly come to a halt. Identification and cataloguing of private investing institutions, their investment objectives, and the
part they play, individually and collectively, in the economic
growth of the country and in the advancement of the living
standards of our society are areas that should be fully covered.

Present projects, research and otherwise, undertaken by industry associations and the like should be reviewed to determine
the extent to which exist overlapping of effort, opportunity for
joint endeavor, and justification for existing functions and services.

Other potential areas for rewarding research include:

1. The discriminatory aspects of tax and other legislation,
including government regulations, as between various branches
of private finance.

2. The significance of the rapidly growing number of institutionally held shares in the ownership of United States industry.

3. In view of the ever-present need for checks on management
and the problems raised for institutional investors in the area
of fiduciary responsibilities versus corporate prerogatives, what
are appropriate standards of conduct and how should they be
developed?

Supplemental Memorandum
Basic Research in the Financial World

Everett G. Judson
Vice President and Director
Keystone Custodian Funds, Inc.

WHEN I referred to discriminations springing from tax treatment or regulation, I had in mind a number of things, of which the following are examples:

Common trust funds, variable annuities, and mutual funds are in direct competition, yet trust funds are regulated by the FRB, variable annuities by state insurance authorities, and mutual funds by the SEC – all following different philosophies, rules, and guidelines. A strong competitive advantage accrues to variable annuity salesmen vis-à-vis mutual funds and common trust funds because of favored tax treatment on current income reinvested. Interest on deposits at mutual savings banks is tax-free under the laws of certain states, while dividend income and bond interest income are not. Commercial banks are regulated by the FRB, savings banks by local bank examiners, and savings and loan associations by the FHMB – once again, all following different policies. I am sure there are more examples, and a compilation and assessment would make an interesting study.

As to Items 2 and 3 in my earlier memorandum (page 148), I might expand along the following lines:

The need for checks on management and performance is ever present, and this becomes a more difficult function as corporations grow larger. The rising dominance of institutional corporate shareholders inevitably entails associated shareholder responsibilities. Reasonably exercised, such action need not be construed as exercising "control." This *is* an obligation since power carries with it responsibility, particularly in the area of corporate programs designed to provide continuity of management. Who is in a better position than the well-staffed institutional investor to evaluate? Isn't this the *all-important* check on management which we must have? The rapidly growing proportion of institutionally held shares in the ownership of United States industry calls for major changes, since present rules and practices were designed for an era when financial institutions did not dominate ownership interests of corporations.

Financial institutions should not sit idly by, particularly as their holdings grow, with the idea that if they become disenchanted with management they will sell. If they do not exercise a responsible influence, certainly the bureaucrats will. Knowledgeable and sophisticated institutional investors have an obligation to develop more profitable corporations – this gets back to management continuity programs – and isn't this the responsible exercise of the institutional investors' corporate franchise, to safeguard portfolio investment?

Let me repeat: What are the appropriate standards of conduct and how should they be developed? Does collective institutional action necessarily mean collusion – control? Bear in mind that the institutional investor is in a position to exert effective influence in the interest of preserving his investment.

Extract from Letter

Albert Y. Bingham
Financial Vice President
Chicago Title and Trust Company

FOR the last year or so I have served on the Research and Publications Committee of the CFA Institute. We have discovered that articles having to do with portfolio management are practically nonexistent. This would indicate that this extremely important field is being handled largely on a subjective basis. Perhaps really basic research could make a vital contribution in this area.

In my opinion, the greatest lack in the area of portfolio management, particularly institutional management, is an adequate yardstick of performance. Years ago the investor of other people's money endeavored to conserve capital and produce a reasonable return. The pendulum has swung so far that today – and this is especially true in mutual fund and pension fund operations – each fund feels that it must produce a better result quarter by quarter or year by year than any other fund, an impossible and quite dangerous objective. It results in much too much money in too few favorites at the same time and produces serious overvaluations.

It has been suggested that performance over a completed cycle is the only fair test. The trouble is that few investment managers live long enough to see many completed cycles. Moreover, during a completed cycle policies and management may have changed so completely that worth-while extrapolation would be impossible.

Performance and risk are intimately related. Innumerable articles have been written on how to value performance, but almost nothing has been said about how much risk was incurred. The problem thus reduces itself to the difficult but essential one of quantifying risk. Then, and only then, can performance be properly measured.

A great deal could be done to improve and increase the investment management services available to the public, the small and medium-sized investor. At present the small investor has virtually no access to the trust companies. He has a choice between going to a broker, whose basic function is to execute orders not provide investment management, or a printed service, frequently of doubtful merit, or taking part in a relatively inflexible plan, such as a common trust fund or a mutual fund.

It has long been a source of concern that commercial banks are given access to almost all figures, budgets, and other data helpful to the management of corporations, whereas most vehicles such as mutual funds and others who handle other people's money are often allowed no information except what is released to all stockholders. Perhaps a valuable research project might be an effort to discover why this sharp difference has become customary. Ordinarily it would seem that a commercial banker who lends for a short period, and often with security, really needs much less information than does the stockholder.

Another subject might be the best way to make capital more readily available to new and small businesses, or to individuals or groups desiring to initiate a business. That the financial community has failed in its responsibility in this area is verified by the fact that the government saw the necessity to create the abortive Small Business Investment Company program. The need for venture capital is particularly great.

Lastly I come to the subject which I think bothers me most. Thanks to what I consider the misguided efforts of the New York Stock Exchange and others, we apparently now have some 18 million to 20 million shareholders in this country. Undoubtedly the fact that we have had a rise in stock prices, only occasionally interrupted, since 1949 has been a large factor, but this in itself could mean a day of reckoning which would seem catastrophic to the vast majority of those shareholders who have never seen a decline, which historically has been normal. Somehow, someway, a method must be developed to protect these people from their own actions. Otherwise the system as we know it will certainly cease to exist. I am not suggesting that we set up some government instrumentality whereby the individual shareholder could be guaranteed against loss, pleasant as that would be, but I am deeply concerned with the political repercussions when such an army of voters, with their dependents, become disillusioned. Obviously, if I knew the answer, research would not be necessary on this or any of the other points I have raised.

Extract from Letter

Carlton R. Copp
Assistant Vice President
The United Corporation

MY SPECIFIC concern, very simply, is this: Is the entry of everyone into everyone else's financial business these days a desirable trend?

In considering this problem I would like to suggest an approach that could provide an orderly and logical method of measuring and evaluating the functions and directions of the various financial media. Basic to this approach is the simple recognition that all financial institutions share one common characteristic. They are all merely *conduits* by which funds accumulating in the hands of savers are channeled into various uses. In one way or another, they all perform their *intermediary* function of allocating savings among the various users pretty much because of established traditional reasons. These reasons and functions should be examined to evaluate how useful and how effective they really are.

It would perhaps seem worth while to use a frame of reference along the lines developed by Bankers Trust, or Salomon Brothers, or others, who prepare detailed *source and disposition of investment funds* data. The "sources" in this case are the financial intermediaries, although, of course, the basic source is personal, business, and, occasionally, government savings. Tables from the 1965 *Investment Outlook* prepared by the Economics Department of Bankers Trust, with which you are probably familiar, could be used as a kind of over-all framework within which to examine the various financial institutions and their present and evolving functions.

This framework might be utilized by first taking the *economic projections* for the economy in the year 1975, as prepared by various government and business-forecasting organizations.

From these economic projections it would be a simple matter to develop projections on the principal *uses* of funds, such as consumer credit, bank loans, corporate bonds, and government securities.

Next, an examination of the potential *sources* of funds for the national economy could be made. It would be interesting to see whether there will be sufficient savings, as things are now going, to provide for these demands, or whether the government will have greatly to extend the credit base artificially to meet its long-term goals.

Assuming that sufficient savings will be generated over the next ten years to provide for these demands for funds, market shares among the various financial institutions could then be projected. These projected sources could be compared with present volume levels among the various financial institutions. It would then be possible to see clearly which were the growth institutions and which existing uses of funds would be expanding most rapidly, and which would perhaps be declining. This then would give some useful data on volume projections for financial intermediaries.

Using this framework of the sources and uses of short-term and investment funds, it would then be possible to measure the *relative cost effectiveness* of the various financial institutions. As a starting point, the present cost of invested capital could be calculated and perhaps projected. With volume data already derived, profit margins, both present and future, could be developed for each institution. Then useful return on invested capital calculations could be made. This return on invested capital approach would show which financial institutions would be most favored in the future and which areas should be promoted through tax or other incentives, or which areas should be avoided and which areas should become less rather than more competitive. It could well develop, for example, that finance companies should get out of the automobile installment credit field because their cost of capital and likely future return on capital will not permit them to compete with the commercial banks, or that the demand for corporate securities will grow so fast that there is plenty of room for participation in the equities field by life insurance companies.

A useful supplementary research area might be a comparison and ranking of all financial intermediaries on the basis of cost and return of capital, perhaps starting with the government, banks, and prime borrowers, and ending with the marginal commercial, financial, or brokerage-type operations. Undoubtedly, some of these, what we might term lower-ranked financial functions, are not really an efficient way of allocating savings resources and could perhaps better be incorporated in the activities of some more efficient financial intermediaries. Knowledge of these figures might actually result – in a free enterprise manner – in a shift in business away from the less-efficient media.

In the event that such an approach was utilized, it could ultimately be extended to include international financial institutions. This would include foreign as well as United States sources and would cover uses of funds in all areas where a free flow of capital is likely to be allowed in the future. This would require the formulation of various economic assumptions and projections for the principal foreign economies. It might indicate, for example, the wisdom of insurance companies, pension plans, and others in following the lead of certain large United States banks in developing significant overseas operations.

The United States
Flow-of-Funds Accounts

C. Stewart Sheppard
Professor of Business Administration,
Graduate School of Business Administration,
University of Virginia,
and Director, The Institute of Chartered Financial Analysts

FACED with a bewildering array of statistical information on the functioning of the national economy, it is understandable that the economist and financial analyst should wish to explore all possibilities for the construction of a realistic framework to integrate national income and product accounts with newer developments in the flow-of-funds accounts. It is difficult at present to move from one set of accounts to the other, but the possibility exists for the correlation of financial and nonfinancial transactions on a plane of consistency that would provide a comprehensive view of both the aggregative economy and its component sectors.

Since 1929 a great deal of work has been done to refine definitions of GNP and related aggregates under the national income and product accounts. The most recent refinement since 1958 is discussed in the August 1965 issue of the *Survey of Current Business*, which outlines the major additions to statistical source data as well as certain changes in the definition of income and product totals and some of their components.

Statistically and conceptually integrated with the national income and product accounts is the 1958 input-output table developed by the United States Department of Commerce. The input-output transactions or flow table for 1958 shows how much of a given industry's output was used by each of the industries of the economy to make its own products and how much was bought by the final purchasers – persons, investors, foreigners, and government. Shown also is the dollar value of each industry's consumption (input) of raw materials, semi-finished products, and services bought from the various industries and the value added – the sum of compensation of employees, profits and proprietors' income, capital consumption allowances, and the like.

The income-product and input-output accounts of the Department of Commerce are concerned mainly with flows of goods and services. On the other hand, the flow-of-funds accounts of the FRS are concerned with financial transactions. Ideally it should be possible to move from one set of accounts to the other in order to analyze relationships between product and financial sectors of the economy. There should be one unified system of national accounts. But a national income accounting system should be so designed that it would relate to either the flow-of-funds or the input-output accounting system. This caveat is underscored by the NBER in its study, *The Flow-of-Funds Approach to Social Accounting*: "Concentrating on just two of the existing forms of national accounts to the exclusion of all the others may create future problems, which could have been avoided by somewhat more forethought at this juncture."

In financial circles there is some excitement over the possibility of meaningful use of the detailed statistical information contained in the flow-of-funds accounts developed by the FRS. Records are available on sources of consumer funds, patterns of consumer expenditures, sources and uses of business funds, banking and monetary statistics, fiscal operations, debt-management policies, and the international balance of payments. And yet these information resources remain largely untapped, as was pointed out by Ritter in his article, "An Exposition of the Structure of the Flow-of-Funds Accounts," in the May 1963 issue of the *Journal of Finance*:

It is now over a decade since Copeland's pioneering work set the stage for what we know today as the flow-of-funds accounts. This was followed in 1955 by the Board of Governors' first exposition of the flow of funds, and then in 1959 by the board's revised presentation. Since then the board has been disgorging statistics at an unbelievable pace, and a few economists have been having a field day discussing the host of technicalities involved.

Meanwhile, the economist who is not a specialist in the capital markets has been sitting uneasily on the sideline, wondering what all the shouting is about and growing increasingly perplexed about what he is to make of this avalanche of numbers that has descended upon him. On occasion he will righteously turn to the *Quarterly Presentation* or to *Supplement 5* and gingerly extract a number, or perhaps even a row of numbers. Other than that, he seems to find little use for the flow of funds in his research and even less use for it in the classroom. If he seeks to orient himself by first acquiring an understanding of the basic framework of the accounts, he will find little help in the literature, most of which is concerned with technical details.

Professor Ritter is entirely justified in his chiding. Apart from the continuing challenge of constructing a macroeconomic model of the functioning of the total economy through integration of product and income accounts, input-output analysis, and flow of funds, there exist the specific challenges to relate flow of funds to corporate sources and uses of funds, to business fluctuations, and to interest rate forecasting.

The flow-of-funds accounts show the financing and borrowing operations of business corporations as a group. In this area the LIAA under O'Leary's direction has developed a continuing series of studies of the demand and supply factors affecting the markets for long-term capital and equity funds and short-term credit. Applications of such studies have been made by commercial banks, life insurance companies, investment counselors, bond houses, and government departments and agencies. Even here ambiguities and inconsistencies persist in flow-of-funds analyses. O'Leary comments in his article entitled, "Application of Flow-of-Funds Data to Capital Market Analysis" in *The Flow-of-Funds Approach to Social Accounting*, a report of the National Bureau of Economic Research published by the Princeton University Press in 1962, as follows:

The Federal Reserve would perform a genuine and

lasting service to the cause of financial knowledge and the spread of general understanding of our financial mechanism if it would use its leadership to develop a basic capital markets statement of accounts which could serve as the standard model or foundation for analysis of trends in the financial fields.

Another interesting application of flow-of-funds accounts is discussed in an article by Atkinson entitled, "Financial Flows in Business Cycles," in the March 1965 issue of the *Journal of Finance*. Admittedly a fragmentary study in the field of economic fluctuations, the article analyzes the occurrence of cyclical regularities in respect to financial assets acquired, assumption of liabilities, and net contribution to or drawing on financial markets by the major sectors of the economy. The conclusion is reached that substantial shifts have occurred in the volume and direction of flow of funds among sectors in postwar cycles, and these shifts in turn are directly related to cyclical changes in income, output, and capital investment and to changes in the level and structure of interest rates.

Increasing attention is being given to the use of flow-of-funds accounts in the forecasting of interest rates. In their article entitled, "Application of Flow-of-Funds to Interest-Rate Forecasting" in the March 1965 issue of the *Journal of Finance*, Freund and Zinbarg concluded:

> If, among the various forecasting techniques examined in this paper, an intuitive approach or some variation thereof is utilized in forecasting some basic interest rate series – say Treasury bills, or long-term governments or Moody's Aaa corporates – it may still be necessary to estimate the probable spreads of other rates in relation to this basic series. For example, mortgage yields may have to be related to bond yields, or municipals to governments. In this endeavor, sector breakdowns of fund flows can be invaluable in suggesting which areas of the money and capital markets will be subject to the greatest relative pressure or ease.

Bankers Trust has circulated interest rate projections within the flow-of-funds framework since the year 1949. In an unpublished doctoral dissertation dated 1965 and entitled, "The Sources and Uses of Funds Approach to Analysis of Interest Rate Developments," Ronk of the Economics Department of Bankers Trust concludes:

> Fundamentally, the effective application of the sources and uses of funds approach to interest rate forecasting is a question of manpower and materials. No one person can possibly be cognizant of every facet of the credit markets. The approach, however, forces the forecaster to examine each slot which is entered into the system in the light of the total picture. This test for consistency provides a discipline which leads to better understanding of the various relationships.

There is much that is inexact and inadequate in the Federal Reserve's flow-of-funds statements, but they hold the promise for a theoretical insight into the total demand for and supply of loanable funds within the economy. There is the future promise of a consistent and logical correlation between statistical data on national income and financial and nonfinancial flows. The imperative need is for concentrated research efforts by economists and financial analysts, first, to acquire understanding of the significance of the raw statistical data and then, and more importantly, to use this data to lend insight into the nature, functioning, and relevance of component sectors of the aggregative economy.

APPENDIX A

The Investment Research Program of the Life Insurance Business

Condensed from the

1964 Record of
Life Insurance Investments

A Report to the Membership
of the
Life Insurance Association of America
by
James J. O'Leary
Vice President and Director of Economic Research

THE following is a report of the progress of the Life Insurance Association's investment research program. This program consists of two main parts, namely, activities of the economic research staff of the LIAA and research sponsored by the Association.

ACTIVITIES OF THE ASSOCIATION'S ECONOMIC RESEARCH STAFF

A major part of the time of the economic research staff is devoted to research on various phases of life insurance investments and the capital markets. Included in this work are such regular annual studies as those of mortgage lending income and costs of life insurance companies, the investment experience of a group of eighteen large life insurance companies in several major classes of bonds and stocks, and the record of life company acquisitions of corporate bonds either by direct placement or public offerings. In addition, the research staff obtains and reports to the life insurance business quarterly data on mortgage loan delinquencies and foreclosures, quarterly data in detail on the various items of cash flow of life companies, monthly data on various classes of forward investment commitments, and monthly data showing the investment yields realized by life insurance companies on direct placements of corporate bonds. The staff likewise prepares and makes available periodic reports on developments in the capital markets, and during the course of the year data are prepared at appropriate intervals showing sources and uses of capital funds in the country as a whole. In addition to these and other studies completed regularly during the course of the year, the economic research staff conducts research devoted to investment policy questions or to questions which have arisen in the legislative area. This year, for example, the staff carried out several pieces of research in connection with possible amendment of the New York law governing life insurance company investments.

In addition to the above research, the staff serves as an economics department for the Association, and in this capacity works with the Joint Economic Policy Committee and its various subcommittees. Frequently this entails the preparation of statements and of investment and economic data which the Joint Economic Policy Committee utilizes in congressional hearings or in meetings with governmental agencies. This year, for example, the staff developed several charts which were employed by the Economic Policy Committee in its discussions in July with United States Treasury officials. In addition, the staff aided in the preparation of a memorandum on monetary policy which was made available to the Federal Reserve authorities. Considerable time of the economic research staff is devoted to working with the Subcommittee on Housing and Mortgage Lending. Here, in particular, is involved the preparation of testimony of the life insurance business in the housing and mortgage lending field in hearings before congressional committees. The Director of Economic Research usually joins the chairman of the Subcommittee in the presentation of testimony before congressional committees. The staff also works with the Joint Subcommittee on Farm Mortgage Lending and the Joint Subcommittee on Transportation Securities.

Through staff work with the Joint Economic Policy Committee and its subcommittees, as well as through the research program, the economic research staff has been a primary point of contact for the life insurance business with a number of government agencies interested in the general economic and investment field, particularly the United States Treasury, the Federal Reserve Board, the Housing and Home Finance Agency, the President's Council of Economic Advisers, and the Bureau of the Budget. These contacts have frequently stemmed from requests which federal agencies have made for information about life insurance investments. This year the Director of Economic Research has served on an advisory committee appointed by the Bureau of the Budget to aid in developing a federal program for obtaining data on mortgage interest rates.

The staff has worked closely, as usual, during the year with the Washington office of the Association in connection with a wide variety of investment and general economic questions affecting the life insurance business. Frequently, of course, this work involves matters of federal legislation.

The economic research staff also performs a staff function for the Joint Committee on Securities and Valuation of Assets. A great deal of our time has been devoted in the past year to servicing this committee, which has been working intensively, as outlined elsewhere in this report, to develop with the National Association of Insurance Commissioners desirable amendments in the NAIC rules governing the valuation of securities held by life insurance companies and the mandatory securities valuation reserves. Our work with the Joint Committee has involved not only research but also the preparation of bulletins to inform the companies of developments and to obtain their reactions. It has also involved extensive contacts and discussions with individual companies as well as with representatives of the NAIC Committee on Valuation of Securities.

More and more in recent years the economic research staff has become a central source of information for the life insurance business on investment, capital market, and general economic questions. This activity is a natural outgrowth of the investment research program as a whole. In this connection, also, the research staff has been utilized as a source of information by other institutions functioning in the investment field, namely, commercial banks, savings banks, pension funds, savings and loan associations, government securities dealers, mortgage bankers, and the like.

RESEARCH FINANCED BY THE ASSOCIATION AS PART OF THE INVESTMENT RESEARCH PROGRAM

In addition to the activities of the economic research staff, the Association sponsors and finances basic economic research of importance to the life insurance business, particularly the investment phase. This research is conducted independently by universities and private research bureaus outside the life insurance business. It is planned and followed closely by the Investment Research Committee of the Association and by the Director of Economic Research. Since 1946 the Board of Directors of the LIAA has approved research grants totaling over $2 million for basic research in the field of finance and the capital markets. These various projects, described and listed below, are widely regarded by scholars and public officials as having been among the most important carried out in this vital area of economic research. They have been conducted by men of outstanding national reputation such as Arthur F. Burns, Raymond J. Saulnier, Raymond Goldsmith, and Simon Kuznets. During the past eighteen years a large number of outstanding economists from all over the country have been involved in our research projects. A summary report on this research follows.

Research Projects That Are in Process.

There are two major projects being sponsored by the Association which are in process of completion and on which good progress has been made this year. These are the Study of Interest Rates and the Study of Tax Policies for Economic Growth.

The Study of Interest Rates.

This project, which was started in 1961 with the aid of a LIAA grant of $318,000, is being conducted by the NBER under the direction of Professor Joseph Conard of Swarthmore College. Last April the Board approved a second grant of $315,000 to continue the project for three more years. An outline of the ground to be covered in this second stage of the study will be presented shortly. It is widely agreed that this project is greatly needed to improve our knowledge of the behavior of interest rates, especially in this period in which interest rates are so much in the public eye.

The objective of this study is to learn what we can about the behavior and determinants of the yields on financial assets. It begins with examination of the factors influencing the movements of yields on specific types of assets and the factors determining the spread between them. The primary emphasis will be upon the behavior of yields in the United States since the

Treasury–Federal Reserve Accord of March 1951, but, when longer coverage can contribute toward an understanding of forces influencing interest rates, exploration will be extended as far back as data permit. The study may also consider rates in other countries in particular instances.

The study consists of four parts. One, the analysis of mortgage yields, is being directed by Dr. Jack Guttentag. The second is an analysis of direct placement yields. This is being conducted by Dr. Avery Cohan. The cyclical behavior of interest rates, though requiring attention in all other parts of the study as well, is the particular subject for an analysis constituting part three of the study. This is being conducted by Dr. Phillip Cagan. The fourth part of the study is an examination of the structures of interest rates in many dimensions and the degree of linkage within the capital markets as revealed by these structures and their changes over time. The dimensions in which rate relations are being studied include type of asset, risk, new versus seasoned issues, coupon rate, call features, term of maturity, and miscellaneous special characteristics, such as tax status. The first characteristic, type of asset, includes at least two major breakdowns: (a) mortgages, bonds, obligations of financial intermediaries, and shares; and (b) debt of the United States government, of state and local governments, and of various kinds of government corporations. Miscellaneous other studies will be included, where required, in order to permit effective analysis of interest rate behavior. Examples are the studies of the seasonal behavior of interest rates and of the spread between yields on new issues and those on outstandings.

In the second stage of the Interest Rate Study, for which the grant of $315,000 was made in April, the NBER is planning the following research and analysis during the next three years. This work will build upon and extend the research and analysis which has already been carried out in the past three years.

1. Further investigation of yields on mortgages. This would involve the development of yield data for 1951–63 on mortgages on income-producing properties, already described above. It would also involve an investigation of the relationship between interest costs and other terms reflecting credit availability, on

the one hand, and the level of construction activity, on the other. Moreover, plans call for further exploration and analysis of currently available data to compare the cyclical behavior of mortgage yields and other interest rates, as well as an analysis of the effects of mortgage costs on residential construction.

2. A pilot study of the linkage between interest rates and real economic activity. This study would be concerned with both the effects of interest rate changes on economic activity and the effects of economic activity on interest rates.

3. A more intensive analysis of the cyclical behavior of interest rates, making use not only of hitherto-published yield data but also of the new data produced in the first phase of the study, e.g., the yields on directly placed corporate bonds and on residential mortgages. The cyclical behavior of interest rates would be related to economic activity generally.

4. Analysis of the linkage of interest rates in the many different financial markets.

5. A study of the changing institutional structure of the money and capital markets and the bearing these changes have upon interest rates. This study would examine changes in existing financial institutions and their practices. It would be essential to an adequate evaluation of the linkages, both within financial markets, on the one hand, and between financial markets and real economic activity, on the other.

The Study of Taxation and Growth.

This study was begun in 1962 with the aid of a grant of $200,000 from the LIAA. It is being conducted by the NBER. Our grant will meet the cost of a study of the effects of *personal income taxation* on incentives to earn, save, and invest, three major aspects of the economic growth process. A companion study by the NBER on the effects of corporate taxation on growth is being financed separately by the Rockefeller Brothers Fund.

The portion of the project being financed by the LIAA is divided into three studies. The first considers the impact of the individual income tax on the amount and character of productive effort. It undertakes to determine the actual level of tax rates and the extent of progression in tax liabilities of certain groups of individuals, such as corporate executives, who are generally regarded as playing a key role in the process of economic growth and who are most likely to be adversely affected by high marginal tax rates. Attempts are being made to ascertain how significantly the actual tax burdens borne by these individuals impinge on their incentives and on the amount and quality of their effort. The initial attention in the study has been devoted to corporate executives, and the study has two main interests: (*a*) to find out how much in the way of rewards corporations have provided for their executives and how progressively these rewards have been taxed; and (*b*) to find out, via interviews with corporate executives, how these executives think that the positions they seek, the tasks they choose to do, and how hard they work at them have been affected by taxation.

The second study is concerned with the effects of the tax treatment of capital gains and losses on personal saving and investment patterns. The basic questions being considered are: (*a*) Does this treatment encourage a higher rate of personal saving by virtue of a greater disposition to save out of capital gains than out of ordinary income? (*b*) Does it encourage individuals to invest in companies with relatively high saving rates, i.e., relatively low dividend distribution rates? (*c*) Does it encourage the allocation of personal saving to relatively risky investment outlets, or is this effect significantly offset by the limitation on the deductibility of capital losses? (*d*) Does the current taxability of gains seriously impede capital transfers by individuals? To investigate these questions, the NBER is using data derived from a continuous sample of identical individuals' income tax returns to the state of Wisconsin, developed at the University of Wisconsin.

The third study deals with the influence of the present tax provisions in regard to income fluctuations. Many types of economic activity deemed to be particularly important in the process of economic growth involve relatively great risk and instability of income over time. A graduated income tax with inadequate provision for averaging fluctuating income and offsetting losses discriminates against such growth-generating activities.

Research Projects Recently Completed.

In addition to the foregoing projects which are under way, it will be useful to review some of the projects completed within the past three years.

The Kuznets Report. Late in 1961 the Princeton University Press published the monograph *Capital in the American Economy: Its Formation and Financing,* prepared by Kuznets of Harvard University. This book, which is the summary volume based on several other reports published earlier by the Princeton University Press, completed a comprehensive study carried out under the NBER with the aid of a grant of $460,000 from the LIAA. Other monographs in this broad study are listed at the end of this section, in an outline of publications growing out of our program.

Kuznets' findings may be summarized as follows: During the period since the Civil War there has been a significant decline in the ratio of the output of capital goods, such as industrial plant and equipment, housing, commercial facilities, and public improvements, to the total output of all goods and services. This is surprising in view of such forces since the Civil War as population growth and technological changes. Kuznets concludes that the available evidence suggests that the force which explains the declining rate of capital formation has been a long-run tendency for the national rate of saving to fall. A major reason for this has been the great expansion of federal spending, which has required a corresponding increase in federal revenues. The sharply rising federal revenue requirements have been met by placing a rising tax burden on individual and corporate incomes, with the over-all effect of cutting the nation's rate of savings. Kuznets holds that at the bottom of much of the rise in the general price level experienced since the end of World War II has been the deficiency of saving relative to capital demands and the fact that this gap has been filled by an expansion of the money supply. Kuznets indicates that if past trends continue, which he expects to be the case, capital demands in the next fifteen years will continue to run ahead of the supply of savings, inflationary pressures will persist, and interest rates will remain very firm. In a country so interested in obtaining a faster rate of economic growth, Kuznets' analysis has tremendously important implications for public policy. One of these is that it is highly important that government policy be directed toward improving the rate of national saving.

Few books have attracted greater attention than Kuznets' monograph. Reviewing it at length in the New York *Times* of December 8, 1961 (p. 1), Lissner stated that Kuznets' "penetrating analysis" showed that "economic growth in recent years has been checked by the limited availability of savings rather than by any shortage of investment opportunities." Kuznets' work has now been widely and favorably reviewed in all of the important journals in the economics profession. It has already been quoted extensively in congressional hearings, especially in hearings before the House Ways and Means Committee on the question of the need for a major cut in federal taxes. There is little doubt that Kuznets' study is the most important one financed thus far under the LIAA investment research program.

The Valuation of Securities Holdings of Life Insurance Companies. This report was prepared by Harold G. Fraine, Professor of Commerce at the University of Wisconsin, and was published in 1962 by Irwin. The product of a three-year study and a grant of $60,000, it analyzes the existing rules of the NAIC regarding the valuation of securities held by life insurance companies and the mandatory securities valuation reserves, and it advances a number of recomendations for modification of these rules. The findings, as noted later in the section of this report entitled "Valuation of Securities," have provided the basis for a thorough reexamination this year of the existing rules by the NAIC regulatory authorities and the industry.

The Value of the Call Privilege. This report was prepared by Professors Arleigh P. Hess, Jr., and Willis J. Winn of the Wharton School of the University of Pennsylvania and was published in 1962 by the University of Pennsylvania Press. It is the product of a three-year study and a grant of $30,000 to the University of Pennsylvania. During the past several years, with flexible interest rates, investors have become more and more conscious of the importance of redemption features in corporate bond financing. The study discusses (*a*) the theoretical value of the call privilege, (*b*) the opinions of institutional investors and regulatory agencies concerning the call privilege, (*c*) call provisions and yields of corporate bonds, 1926–59, (*d*) the call feature in government financing, mortgage loans, and leases, and (*e*) the effect of redemption provisions upon the flow of funds into corporate financing. Two of the important conclusions reached in the report are that from a theoretical viewpoint the value of the call privilege in a period of high interest rates would be greater than actual experience indicates has been the case, and that there is an increasing awareness on the part of investors of the importance of call protection. The report has been valuable as a means of calling the attention of investors, the SEC, and other regulatory authorities, to the significance of redemption features in corporate financing.

The Secondary Mortgage Market. This report was prepared by Oliver Jones and Professor Leo Grebler of the University of California at Los Angeles and was published in 1962 by the University of California Press. The study was financed jointly by the LIAA, the United States Savings and Loan League, and the National Association of Mutual Savings Banks, with a two-year grant of $60,000, of which the LIAA contribution was $45,000. For the past few years the adequacy of the secondary mortgage market in the United States has been a lively subject for congressional consideration. The purpose of this study was to analyze and appraise the functioning of the secondary mortgage market and to review the steps which have been taken, as well as those proposed, to make the secondary market more effective. The first part of the report analyzes the mortgage market of today and discusses the structure of the market, its performance record, and the broad economic consequences of its record. The second part considers the Federal National Mortgage Association and the effects of FNMA's activities. The third part outlines a number of reforms needed to strengthen both the primary and secondary mortgage market. This report has received a great deal of attention from students of housing and mortgage lending and from congressional committees. It should play an important role in discussions of the secondary mortgage market which will occur in the next session of Congress.

A list of the publications growing out of research sponsored by the LIAA's investment research program since its inception in 1947, as well as reports in an advanced stage of preparation, follows:

  I. *A Study of Saving in the United States,* by Goldsmith. 3v. Princeton University Press, 1955–1956.
 II. *The Study of Capital Formation and Financing* (Conducted by the NBER under Kuznets).
    A. Monographs published by Princeton University Press.
      1. *Capital Formation in Residential Real Estate: Trends and Prospects*, by Grebler, Blank, and Winnick. 1956.
      2. *Capital in Agriculture: Its Formation and Financing since 1870*, by Tostlebe. 1957.
      3. *Financial Intermediaries in the American Economy since 1900*, by Goldsmith. 1958.
      4. *Capital in Transportation, Communications, and Public Utilities: Its Formation and Financing*, by Ulmer. 1960.
      5. *Capital in Manufacturing and Mining: Its Formation and Financing,* by Creamer, Dobrovolsky, and Borenstein. 1960.
      6. Trends in Government Financing, by Copeland. 1961.
      7. *Capital in the American Economy: Its Formation and Financing*, by Kuznets. 1961.
    B. Occasional papers published by Princeton University Press
      1. *The Role of Federal Credit Aids in Residential Construction,* by Grebler (no. 39).

2. *Capital and Output Trends in Manufacturing Industries, 1880–1948*, by Creamer (no. 41).
3. *The Share of Financial Intermediaries in National Wealth and National Assets, 1900–1949*, by Goldsmith (no. 42).
4. *Trends and Cycles in Capital Formation by United States Railroad, 1870–1950*, by Ulmer (no. 43).
5. *The Growth of Physical Capital in Agriculture, 1870–1950*, by Tostlebe (no. 44).
6. *Capital and Output Trends in Mining Industries, 1870–1948*, by Borenstein (no. 45).
7. *The Volume of Residential Construction, 1889–1950*, by Blank (Technical paper no. 9).

III. *The Study of the Postwar Capital Markets* (Conducted by the NBER).
   A. Monographs published by Princeton University Press.
      1. *The Postwar Market for State and Local Government Securities*, by Robinson. 1960.
      2. *The Postwar Residential Mortgage Market*, by Klaman. 1961
   B. Papers published by Princeton University Press.
      1. *The Postwar Rise of Mortgage Companies*, by Klaman (Occasional paper no. 60).
      2. *The Volume of Mortgage Debt in the Postwar Decade*, by Klaman (Technical paper no. 13).
      3. *United States Savings Bond Program in the Postwar Period*, by Hanc (Occasional paper no. 81).
      4. *The Measurement of Corporate Sources and Uses of Funds*, by Shapiro and Meiselman (Technical paper no. 18).
   C. Manuscripts in advanced stage of preparation
      1. Monographs
         a. "The Flow of Capital Funds in the Postwar Economy," by Goldsmith.
         b. "The Market for Corporate Securities and Loans," by Shapiro.

IV. *Corporate Earning Power and Market Valuation, 1935–1955*, by Cottle and Whitman. Duke University Press, 1959.

V. *Corporate Bond Project* (Financial Research Program).

  A. Monographs published by Princeton University Press.

    1. *The Volume of Corporate Bond Financing since 1900*, by Hickman. 1953.

    2. *Corporate Bond Quality and Investor Experience*, by Hickman. 1958.

    3. *Statistical Measures of Corporate Bond Financing since 1900*, by Hickman. 1960.

  B. Occasional paper published by Princeton University Press.

    1. *Corporate Bonds: Quality and Investment Performance,* by Hickman. 1957.

VI. *Other Published Studies.*

  A. *Investment Timing: The Formula Plan Approach*, by Cottle and Whitman. McGraw-Hill, 1953.

  B. *The Mutual Mortgage Insurance Fund,* by Fisher and Rapkin. Columbia University Press, 1956.

  C. *Economic Aspects of Atomic Power*, by Schurr and Marschak. Princeton University Press, 1950.

  D. *Valuation of Securities Holdings of Life Insurance Companies,* by Fraine. Richard D. Irwin, Inc., 1962.

  E. *The Value of the Call Privilege*, by Hess and Winn. University of Pennsylvania Press, 1962.

  F. *The Secondary Mortgage Market*, by Jones and Grebler. University of California Press, 1962.

APPENDIX B

Research in the Capital Markets

Condensed from

a report with the same title

by the

National Bureau Exploratory Committee
on Research in the Capital Markets in
the *Journal of Finance,*
Vol. XIX, Sup. (May 1964), No. 2, Part 2

(An Exploratory Report by the
National Bureau of Economic Research)

I. INTRODUCTION

THIS is the fourth report of an exploratory committee on financial research to be issued during the past quarter of a century. The first report, *A Program of Financial Research,* was published in 1937. It was followed in 1946 by *Research in Securities Markets* and in 1954 by *Research in the Capital and Securities Markets.* The present report concentrates principally on the capital markets. Like the others, it is the product of a broadly based exploratory committee established under the auspices of the NBER. The purposes of the Committee were twofold: to survey the present state of knowledge of the capital markets and, on the basis of its findings, to recommend directions in which further research would be most fruitful.

In surveying the state of knowledge in 1937, as a basis from which to recommend priorities for further research, the Committee found that there was a lack of any conception of the most elementary magnitudes involved in the financial structure.

It is obvious to even a cursory observer of the financial scene that matters have improved greatly since issuance of the report quoted above. One has only to mention the continuous stream of data emanating from the Federal Reserve's flow-of-funds section, Kuznets' *Capital in the American Economy: Its Formation and Financing* (1961), Goldsmith's monumental *A Study of Saving in the United States* (1955–56), his *Financial Intermediaries in the American Economy since 1900* (1958), his *The National Wealth of the United States in the Postwar Period* (1962), and his joint work with Lipsey, *Studies in the National Balance Sheet of the United States* (1963), to realize that, for sheer data and information on financial institutions and practices, we are incomparably better off than we were a quarter century ago. These works, along with many others from university scholars, government agencies, and private research organizations, now provide us with a body of knowledge on the functioning of our financial system which is undoubtedly superior to that available in any other country in the world. Furthermore, this knowledge has been growing at a rapid rate in recent years; indeed, most of it has been accumulated in the last decade.

This does not mean, however, that there is no need for further research in this field. There are still significant gaps in the available data, as well as a pressing need for the interpretation of the existing data. These topics are the concern of the present document. The recommendations which emerged from the discussions in the Exploratory Committee on identifying the areas most in need of further research are presented in Parts II and III below. Part II is concerned with research topics which encompass the capital market as a whole, and Part III with narrower sectors within the capital market, corresponding roughly to the conventional classification of sectors by type of market instrument.

As a basis for forming its judgments, the Committee first surveyed the status of recent research in the field, including that currently in progress or planned. This "inventory" is presented in Part IV, in the hope that it will provide a helpful checklist for others.

Before turning to the research recommendations, a word is in order about the general orientation of the report. In the first place, in exploring the needs for further research in the capital markets, the Committee attempted to keep the scope of its inquiry within manageable proportions by confining itself primarily to financial markets, in contrast to factor and product markets. In the financial markets, it concentrated mainly on intermediate and long-term financing, in contrast to flows of short-term funds.

At the same time, there was full awareness that financial markets cannot actually be separated from the markets for goods and services and that flows of intermediate and long-term funds are intimately connected with flows of short-term funds. Aspects of these relationships are thus found among the Committee's recommendations. The fact that there is not more on the "real" aspects of economic activity, or on short-term financial markets, does not imply that knowledge in these areas is adequate; it simply reflects the definition of the scope of the report.

Second, no attempt has been made to specify an order of priorities among the research projects recommended below. In a general way, most of the Committee members felt that the topics in Part II were more important than those in Part III, i.e., that analysis of the capital market as a whole deserved priority over more intensive work on any one sector within that market. The report lists the research areas we think need further exploration; the reader is free to assign to them any priorities he believes appropriate.

Third, it is worth noting that there was a strong feeling within the Committee – which is reflected in its recommendations – that the time had come to emphasize analysis and interpretation instead of the accumulation of additional data.   For whereas an imposing body of facts and figures has been accumulated on the capital markets in the past decade, there has been much less interpretation of these data. This does not, of course, mean that we already have all the data we need; there are still many areas, as indicated below, where analysis is hampered by inadequate factual knowledge. But in other areas it is imperative that the opposite imbalance be redressed and that more emphasis be placed on the consolidation, interpretation, and analysis of data already at hand.

Fourth, the Committee feels that the research recommended below would have the maximum impact if it were directed, as far as possible, toward illuminating the major economic issues encountered in the formulation and execution of public policy. This would involve outlining alternative courses of action and consideration of their possible consequences. Theoretical and empirical analyses of current relationships and prospective tendencies, as well as the development of historical perspective, are of course essential ingredients in policy-oriented research. But the full value of the insights gained will not be realized unless their bearing on controversial aspects of current policy problems is made clear. Although this is frequently hazardous, the Committee strongly feels that the results would be worth the effort in terms of professional contribution to an informed consideration of the issues in question.

Fifth, it is not contemplated that the various projects proposed here will be undertaken by any single group or institution. On the contrary, it is the Committee's hope that this report will stimulate research in the capital markets in many quarters and by many people.

Finally, it should be understood that this report is the product of the Committee as a whole. Within the Committee opinions differed as to the value of individual research projects. Every member of the Committee does not therefore necessarily endorse each and every recommendation made in the following pages.

II. RECOMMENDATIONS FOR
FURTHER RESEARCH:
THE CAPITAL MARKET AS A WHOLE

1. Role of the Capital Market in Attaining National Economic Objectives

With the information on the capital markets we now have, it is time to focus our research on the way the operations of these markets affect the broad economic problems of our times. For example, how does the functioning of the capital market facilitate or hinder the national economic objectives of economic growth, price stability, high-level employment, efficient resource allocation, and balance of payments equilibrium? Does our experience have any implications for the presently underdeveloped countries? Could any broad generalizations be made from the economic history of this and other countries which would throw light on the influence of the capital markets on economic growth and stability?

Among the many topics relevant in this connection is a thoroughgoing comparison of the capital markets in a number of countries in different stages of economic development. This should include their form of organization, their principal financial institutions, the nature and scope of governmental regulation, conventional modes of behavior, the degree of mobility of funds, and the like.

Of similar value would be a large-scale attempt to draw up

projections of saving, investment, and flows of funds from ultimate lenders directly or through financial institutions to ultimate borrowers over the next decade or two in the United States.

2. Role of Government in the Capital Markets

Throughout this report suggestions are made for explorations of the impact of government regulation on *specific* sectors of the capital market. To do justice to this subject, however, there is need for a broad examination of the role of government influence on the functioning of the financial system *as a whole*. Our capital markets operate within an all-pervasive legal, regulatory, and tax framework which has grown up in a haphazard and unsystematic fashion. A critical examination of the impact of these legal and regulatory influences, on an over-all basis, is long overdue. It should cover regulations on competition among financial institutions and on portfolio policies, regulations affecting flows of funds to alternative markets, tax influences, and the like.

3. Interrelations among Sectors of the Capital Market

If corporate bond flotations rise, to what extent and how rapidly does this affect yields in the market for state and local government securities? If corporate bond yields rise, to what extent and how rapidly does this affect the supply of new corporate stocks? A great deal of research has been done on particular segments of the capital market, taken separately, but not nearly as much has been done on the capital market taken as a single entity. Our knowledge is inadequate about the interrelations among the sectors of the capital market, the way changes in one market are transmitted to the others, the extent of such changes, and the speed of transmission.

4. Portfolio Decision-Making and the Liquidity and Transferability of Financial Assets

Continued economic growth, vigorous competition in financial markets, and rising levels of income have contributed to a proliferation of the types of financial assets held by consumers and businesses, and to a relatively larger increase in claims on nonbank financial intermediaries than on banks. Virtually all of these claims are in some degree substitutes for money balances, and all possess some degree of liquidity in the minds of their holders. An integrated set of studies is needed of the factors determining the composition and magnitude of such holdings, the influence of such holdings upon the economic actions of their owners, and the actual liquidity of the instruments (including equities) which our market mechanism provides. The project could be coordinated with the recent explorations of the Cowles Foundation in analyzing the financial behavior of individuals and institutions (see 6 below).

5. Influence of Financial Markets on Real Expenditures

Although the role of financial markets in influencing real expenditures has been the focus of a number of recent studies, particularly those sponsored by the Commission on Money and Credit, remarkably little progress has been made in understanding the relationships involved. Among the major issues are the cyclical influence of interest rates and credit conditions in general on various forms of borrowing and spending and the interrelations between financial and real variables in various sectors of the economy (both cyclical influences and resource allocation).

For example, do financial variables merely adjust to changes in "real" phenomena, or do they influence the behavior of real variables? If the latter, to what extent? Intensive application of the flow-of-funds accounts should be made to seek answers to such issues.

6. Comparative Studies of Financial Institutions and Market Structures

The Committee did not consider the subject of financial institutions per se within its purview. Nevertheless, it is obvious that the growth and behavior of financial institutions exert a powerful impact on the functioning of the capital markets; to that extent their behavior is pertinent to the interests of the

Committee. The American financial fabric comprises many different types of institutions, a goodly number of which originally were adapted to special circumstances and accordingly endowed with specialized powers. During the postwar period there have been marked changes in the relative importance of, and some changes in the functions performed by, the major types of institutions; it is evident that still further changes are currently in process. Accordingly, it is important to document these recent changes and assess their relevance to the issue of special-purpose versus general-purpose institutions. Particular issues which should be examined are the criteria that might be used in assessing the optimum degree of specialization among financial institutions, the extent to which our institutional structure falls short of the optimum, and the tendency of that structure on balance to improve or deteriorate in the period under review.

7. Integration of National Income and Flow-of-Funds Accounts

Thanks to the Department of Commerce and the Board of Governors of the FRS, the United States has excellent data in the national income and the flow-of-funds accounts. However, it is extremely clumsy and awkward for users to move from one set of accounts to the other. The income and product accounts of the Department of Commerce are concerned exclusively with flows of goods and services, whereas the flow-of-funds accounts of the Federal Reserve are concerned primarily with financial transactions. It should be possible to move quickly and easily between the two, in order to examine the crucial relationships between the real and financial sectors of the economy. In brief, the accounts should be integrated into a unified whole. To suggest this is in no sense to disparage the value of the accounts as they are now constructed. Indeed, the flow-of-funds data promise to accelerate progress in capital market analysis in ways impossible only a decade ago. But improvements can still be made, and in the minds of the Committee the greatest need is for a rearrangement of the accounts into a single integrated pattern.

8. Measurement and Flow of Saving

At least three projects in this area are of major importance. First, data on saving now emanate from several different sources: the Department of Commerce, the Board of Governors of the FRS, the Federal Home Loan Bank Board, and the SEC. Each defines the concept somewhat differently, so that the various saving series often behave differently over the cycle. A project exploring the reasons for the different cyclical behavior of the various saving series, and the implications of the differences, would be of great value. Consideration should also be given to continuing, and possibly revising, the long-term estimates of saving made by Goldsmith in his *A Study of Saving*. A segment of such a project might be devoted to the conceptual and statistical difficulties involved in the frequent comparison between financing "out of saving" compared with financing "by monetary creation." The conceptual distinction between these two is not always as clear as it might be, nor are the implications for their impact on the economy.

Second, useful work could be done on the differential rates of growth of savings at various types of financial institutions, and the characteristics and motivations influencing depositors at each. An important issue here involves the interest elasticity (as well as convenience and availability elasticity) of financial savings as determinants of the type of savings facility selected by households. While economists have concerned themselves intensively with the response or lack of response of aggregative savings to changing interest rate levels, very little work has been done on the response to differential interest rates and other conveniences and facilities offered by different financial intermediaries. We know, of course, that location, convenience, selling effort, and images of relative safety, as well as interest rates, are important determinants of savings, but beyond such generalities our knowledge is extremely limited.

Finally, more work needs to be done on the measurement of flows of financial saving. At present we get little information on gross financial saving flows – such as gross deposits and gross withdrawals – and instead only a figure for net change. Gross data might reveal tendencies and relationships not discernible from net figures, especially with respect to the influence of interest rates and other variables on financial flows. Incidentally, this observation applies equally well to other markets – bonds, mortgages, loans, and the like. Such data might be classified by category of savers, geographic area, occupation of individuals, and type of institutions. In addition, the effect of compound interest on savings accruals should be distinguished from inputs of new funds.

9. Quality of Credit

The issues of credit quality, its cyclical changes, and its influence on economic activity cut across many areas of the capital markets. For mortgage credit, for example, preliminary data as revealed in Earley's progress reports in the Quality of Credit Program suggest that the quality of mortgage credit may be deteriorating, perhaps more so than any other sector of the capital market. The quality standards of different types of mortgage lenders should be examined, as well as the supervisory and legal safeguards which regulate the activities of various types of lenders. The relationship between mortgage quality and yield, default experience, cyclical and secular variations in quality standards, and related matters are all worthy of investigation. Commercial as well as residential mortgages should, of course, be included. A thorough study of secondary financing of residential properties, in all their various forms, would also fit in well with such a quality of credit project.

Similarly, a substantial gap in our knowledge of the functioning of the municipal bond market is due to the lack of data on the quality of state and local government credit, including the relationship between quality and yield and the cyclical and secular behavior of the quality of state and local credit.

Finally, the evidence available thus far seems to indicate that there has been no deterioration in the quality of foreign securities, but a closer look might be useful in view of experience during the 1920's and 1930's.

III. RECOMMENDATIONS FOR FURTHER RESEARCH:
PARTICULAR SECTORS OF THE CAPITAL MARKET

A. *The Markets for Corporate Securities*

At the end of 1962 the market value of outstanding corporate stock amounted to over $600 billion, well over 40 percent of the total of all outstanding credit and equity market instruments. Corporate bonds, actually the favored method of postwar external corporate finance relative to stock financing, totaled over $100 billion. The Committee feels, particularly in view of the magnitude of these figures, that our knowledge of the functioning of these markets, especially the market for equities, could be substantially improved. One bright spot on the horizon is the substantial volume of recent research and research currently under way into various aspects of the stock market. It is to be hoped that these research efforts, and research along the lines indicated below, will help to remedy the present serious deficiencies in our knowledge.

What is really needed in the equities market is a full-scale historical and analytical exploration of the flow of funds through equity channels, including the secondary market, the new-issues market, the over-the-counter market, local and informal arrangements, and the organized securities exchanges. Who does the buying, and for what reasons? Who are the sellers, and why? What forces are significant in the determination of stock prices? How does the efficiency of the over-the-counter market compare with the organized exchanges? What cyclical and secular influences are evident? Finally, enough up-to-date data should be provided to permit the continuation of the analysis on a current basis. The specific research recommendations which follow are designed, when taken together and in conjunction with other current research, ultimately to achieve these objectives.

1. *Demand for Equities*

Who are the buyers of stocks including new issues and outstanding shares? Could this information be obtained annually or even quarterly? A great deal of work needs to be done on the determinants of stock ownership, on risk-taking attitudes of major purchasers, on the role of expectations in this market, and on the reasons for cyclical and secular changes in the distribution of stock ownership.

2. Supply of Equities

For the secondary market, explorations of risk attitudes and better data on cyclical and secular shifts in ownership would obviously throw light on the supply side as well as the demand side. In addition, special work could fruitfully be done on the role of the estate tax in expanding the market supply of equities through forced sales and on institutional policies toward disposing of securities.

Data on the new-issues market are also inadequate.

3. Investor Experience with Common Stocks

A reading of Hickman's volumes on the Corporate Bond Research Project (see 11 below) leads one to wish that something along similar lines might be done for common stocks. The design of such a study should be broad in scope and cover a considerable time period. It should endeavor to determine the experience of investors with common stocks during successive time periods, in the aggregate and by industry classifications, as well as by other characteristics. It would be extremely useful to examine the ex post facto results of investments in equities of different quality or other characteristics. Yields after losses, including capital gains, might be studied as a function of risk. In addition, it would be useful to study the behavior of return on equities over time as contrasted with yields on bonds. An analysis of the behavior of the differentials might be extremely revealing. An interesting subsection of this study could be to examine the meaning of "return" on a stock: dividend-price ratio, earnings-price ratio, rate of capital gain, and the like. It is to be hoped that the University of Chicago's current stock market study (see 9 below) will fill a number of these gaps.

4. Economics of the Securities Industry

The Committee is reluctant to recommend further large-scale research in this area in view of the recent report of the SEC.

Recommendations will necessarily have to await evaluation of the considerable analysis and body of data contained in the SEC study report on brokers and dealers, market making in the over-the-counter market, commission rates, and similar topics. Furthermore, as a result of the report, there may be some changes in the data gathering of the SEC in this field.

However, although many of the questions raised below are discussed in the SEC report, it is rather surprising that in the past we have had so little systematic knowledge about the securities industry *as an industry* or about securities brokers and dealers *as business firms.*

5. Comparison between Listed and Over-the-Counter Markets

The Committee believes that an analysis of the performance of listed and over-the-counter securities markets would be of substantial value. How do the listed markets compare with the over-the-counter markets in efficiency of operation, price fluctuation, ease of transfer, depth, and resiliency? It is usually assumed that an organized auction market is superior to an over-the-counter negotiated market for the shares of large non-financial business corporations. On the other hand, the government bond market is an efficient over-the-counter market, and insurance companies and banks have generally avoided listing. A study of the relative advantages and disadvantages of each type of market – for different types of securities and for various sizes of issuers – can now be undertaken with more adequate data and background information than were available before the completion of the SEC study.

6. Investment Banking and the New-Issues Market

Because of the full-scale studies now under way at the Wharton School, and those recently completed by the SEC, including studies of the over-the-counter markets, the Committee is reluctant to recommend large-scale research in these fields at the present time. It is worth mentioning in passing, however, that the intrastate distribution of and dealing in new issues deserve further examination. Chapter IV of the SEC's Special Study of Securities Markets discusses this problem and makes recommendations for legislation. State regulatory statutes vary and the effectiveness of enforcement varies even more. In some instances, state laws seem to constrain rather severely the intra-state distribution of small companies, and in other states extreme laxity seems to prevail.

The arrangements between originators and dealers, also selling and pricing techniques, deserve systematic analysis.

7. *Determinants of Stock Prices*

In addition to bringing the data and analysis of the projects mentioned above to bear on the determinants of stock values, such interrelated empirical and analytical inquiries as the following would be relevant as well as important in their own right: the relationship between stock prices and economic activity; the influence of the money supply, wealth, and interest rates on stock prices; the relationships between risk, marketability, and rate of return; the empirical relationshps between profits, cash flow, dividends, and stock prices; the underlying reasons for differential rates of discount of future revenue streams by different investors and trends and cycles therein; trends and cycles in corporate debt-equity ratios by sectors and their influence on stock prices; the effects of changes in stock prices on methods of corporate finance. Such an inquiry would not only augment our understanding of the determination of stock prices, but would simultaneously contribute an empirical base relevant to the growing theoretical literature on the cost of funds, financial economies of scale, corporate capital structure, and related matters in corporation finance.

B. *Mortgage Market*

1. *Market for Multifamily and Commercial Mortgages*

By far the greater part of research in the mortgage market ha been confined to single-family residential mortgages, with t' result that our knowledge of the operation of that market exceeds our knowledge of multi-family residential and residential commercial mortgage financing practices. Nor *commercial* mortgages, for example, amounted to $33 bil' the end of 1960, 15 percent of total outstanding mortgages. Nevertheless, we have very little information on how this market functions. We are aware, however, that it functions very differently from the residential mortgage market. In Gold-smith's words:

> In view of the size and importance of that [non-residential nonfarm mortgage] market the degree of our lack of relevant statistics and the almost complete absence of analysis of what happens in that market is truly astonishing. Not the least to be gained from reading a description and analysis of the market for residential mortgages, which Klaman's book pro-vides, is the realization of how great is the need for a similar study of the market for nonresidential non-farm mortgages.[1]

2. Secondary Mortgage Market

The future significance of the growth of a more highly developed secondary mortgage market should be explored for its implications for flows of funds, institutional and individual portfolio management, and the allocation of real resources. As a prelude to such a study, we need better information on the nature and extent of the secondary mortgage market today. For instance, to what extent is it confined to government-under-written mortgages? What is the current magnitude of this market, and how has it been changing in recent years?

C. Market for State and Local Government Securities

x-Exemption Privilege

years the special tax treatment of interest on municipal has been a topic of heated and often emotional debate. gh several notable studies have been made, the surface ely been scratched. Alternative assumptions about in-ehavior, tax rates, and other factors lead to different

---

(Pr₁ to Saul B. Klaman, *The Postwar Residential Mortgage Market* niversity Press for NBER, 1961), p. xxv.

conclusions on the likely effects of removing the tax-exemption feature. A thoroughgoing, impartial, analytical and empirical analysis of the full range of alternatives involved would be helpful, particularly in view of the recent sharp growth of industrial aid revenue bonds. Indeed, that growth itself, as well as the issues involved in using tax-exempt municipal bonds to help finance private industrial plants, deserves thorough study. Most recently the advance refunding of revenue bonds has raised related questions.

2. Historical and Current Data

There are four notable gaps in the available data which it would be desirable to fill: first, historical yield data by maturity classes; second, detailed information on ownership, preferably a quarterly or even monthly series of ownership, by maturity breakdown; third, data on the volume of trading in the municipal market; and fourth, data on retirements of state and local securities.

D. Market for Federal Government Securities

Of all the sectors of the capital market, we undoubtedly have the most complete information on the functioning of the market for federal government securities. In addition, current and historical data on yields, ownership, and related matters are as complete as one could expect. We know how many securities have been issued, of what type, and at what yields, with reasonable accuracy. Shifts of ownership are also fairly traceable, although even here an ownership breakdown within the present large "all other" category would be extremely helpful.

This abundance of factual information provides a solid basis for research directed toward finding workable solutions to the pressing problems of public policy in this area.

1. Extent of Market Segmentation and Substitutability

A crucial question at the heart of much of the controversy on debt management, and also closely involved in the recent monetary policy dispute about "bills only," is the extent to which purchasers of government securities are willing and able to shift funds into and out of such securities.

2. Debt Management and Flows of Funds through the Financial System

In 1959 market rates on short-term government securities rose above the interest rates on deposits at most savings institutions. The result was said to be a sharp disruption of flows to savings institutions as the public shifted dramatically to the higher-yielding alternatives. The implications of this experience – in the effects on flows of funds through the financial system, on forward commitments of savings institutions, and on the direction of real expenditures – deserve more thorough exploration and analysis than they have received thus far. Broad issues are involved in the kind of thoroughgoing Treasury competition for long- and short-term funds which is often recommended.

3. Speed of Reaction to Changes in Debt Structure

The time lag between debt-management decisions and consequent alterations in the level and structure of interest rates, the volume and direction of financial flows, and ultimately the level and pattern of real expenditure is a subject which remains largely unexplored. Quite aside from the magnitude of these effects, it is important to have some idea of the speed with which they take place and the factors important in determining that speed. It also may be relevant, for such time lags, whether changes in the debt structure take place because of actions of the Treasury or because of actions undertaken by the Federal Reserve. The nature of the institutional arrangements are such that the initial action will take place through somewhat different market channels, involving perhaps different market expectations, depending on the agency responsible, thereby producing different results.

E. Market for Foreign Securities

The United States is now widely recognized as the leading financial center for international capital market transactions.

The volume of long-term foreign securities floated here – and the volume of long-term American securities sold to foreigners – had reached substantial proportions before the interest equalization tax was proposed in mid-1963, so much so that it directly affected public policy and promises to continue to do so indefinitely. Nevertheless, we know relatively little about the operation of this segment of the capital market, which is rather surprising since so much discussion of public policy in this area necessarily involves assumptions about the nature and characteristics of this market. It is possible that our lack of understanding of its technical structure and functioning may be leading us to incorrect conclusions about the determinants of international capital flows, both short- and long-term, and hence to inappropriate public policies.

For these reasons the Committee believes that high priority attaches to systematic and fundamental research into the nature and implications of international financial markets and flows of funds. This involves, of course, not one but several markets: the United States market for new foreign issues, the United States market for outstanding securities of foreign issuers (especially foreign common stocks), term loans to foreigners, the foreign market for new United States issues, and the foreign market for outstanding securities of United States firms. Also included should be so-called "soft loans" and their effects on the balance of payments. Among the important matters requiring clarification are the following:

1. Basic Data on Demand, Supply, and Prices

Who buys the securities? What legal factors, including legal restrictions on institutional purchase, are in effect? Who sells the securities (private or governmental borrowers), and at what yields? It would be helpful to have comprehensive yield and ownership data for at least five years back. Regarding ownership, it is important to find out how many of the foreign flotations are "permanently" lodged here and how many are not, i.e., how much of what appears to be tapping our savings stream is actually tapping foreign funds temporarily lodged in the United States. Term loans to foreigners are also an important area of inquiry.

2. Market Characteristics and Facilities

The SEC could usefully publish data on the proportion of foreign securities privately placed and publicly floated. Further questions that should be investigated are: Who does the underwriting, and at what cost? What is the volume of trading in the secondary market, and who makes markets in these issues? What legal and tax factors are involved? How do the institutional facilities here compare with similar facilities abroad? A comparative analysis of the structure of the money and capital markets here and abroad may throw light on many of the factors underlying international flows of funds.

3. Determinants of Foreign Flotations in the United States and Domestic Borrowing Abroad

The following factors should be examined: the influence of interest rates, credit availability, and other market conditions in United States capital markets on the volume of foreign borrowing here and on the volume of foreign purchases of United States securities; the role of business conditions here and abroad; tax factors; stock prices; profits; cyclical and secular trends; and the like. Of particular interest, of course, is the relative importance of interest rate differentials, both long- and short-term.

IV. AN INVENTORY OF RECENT AND CURRENT RESEARCH

Since the publication of the 1954 Exploratory Committee Report, a substantial volume of research has been conducted in capital markets. As a prelude to recommending the topics most in need of further research, where the gaps in our knowledge are most serious, the Committee necessarily had to assess the present state of our knowledge. To this end, a survey was made of recent research (since 1954), and interested parties were contacted for information on research currently in progress or in the planning stage.

There are fifteen large-scale projects which are producing important monographs. The fact that there are fifteen attests to the scope and vigor with which research has been pursued in this field in recent years and is being pursued today.

1. The National Bureau's Study of Capital Formation and Financing in the United States.

Under the general direction of Simon Kuznets, this project was begun in 1950, with the aid of a grant from the LIAA, and was completed in 1961 with the publication of Kuznets' summary volume, *Capital in the American Economy: Its Formation and Financing.*

The project as a whole examined long-term trends in capital formation in terms of the principal capital-using sectors of the economy: agriculture, mining and manufacturing, the regulated industries, nonfarm residential real estate, and governments. The analysis for each sector summarized the major trends in real capital formation since 1870, or the earliest year for which data were available, and in financing since 1900. Also explored were the implications for the future of past trends in saving and investment.

2. The National Bureau's Postwar Capital Markets Study.

Under the general direction of Raymond W. Goldsmith, this project was begun in 1955 with a grant from the LIAA. It will be summarized in Goldsmith's forthcoming *The Flow of Capital Funds in the Postwar Economy.* The project as a whole presents the main features of the American capital market for 1945–58, primarily in terms of flows of funds.

Also under the general direction of Goldsmith, and indeed a part of the Postwar Capital Markets Study, are the NBER's studies in national wealth and national balance sheets. To a large extent these data formed the basis for much of the analysis of the postwar capital markets. Included are national and sector balance sheets and estimates of tangible wealth for 1945–58, carrying forward similar estimates available for prior years in Goldsmith's *Study of Saving.*

3. The Federal Reserve's Flow-of-Funds Research.

On the basis of Morris A. Copeland's pioneering *Study of Moneyflows in the United States* (NBER, 1952), the Board of

Governors has developed its set of annual accounts and quarterly accounts. Recently, seasonally adjusted quarterly data have been released. Most recent capital markets research is directly or indirectly dependent upon the flow-of-funds accounts. Closely connected with this is the current work at the Federal Reserve on consumer financial characteristics.

4. Commission on Money and Credit.

The Commission on Money and Credit was established under the auspices of the Committee for Economic Development in 1958 and was sponsored largely by the Ford Foundation. The purpose was to conduct a thorough examination of our financial system and to make recommendations for public policy. It issued its report in 1961 and since then has been releasing the background papers prepared by scholars for the use of the Commission.

5. The Harvard Capital Markets Study.

Begun in 1959, the Harvard project is under the general supervision of James S. Duesenberry, Eli Shapiro, and Lawrence E. Thompson. Its broad objective is to explain how the major demands for funds and the supply of funds have been brought into balance in the postwar period in United States capital markets. Ultimately this is expected to involve a simultaneous analysis of the whole network of capital market interactions, but thus far the major effort has been devoted to gathering data on the behavior of key transactors.

6. The Cowles Foundation Program in Financial Research, Yale University.

Under the general direction of James Tobin, the Cowles Foundation has been extremely active in financial research in recent years, exploring financial institutions and capital markets and their relation to economic fluctuations and growth. The basic Cowles approach is twofold: first, the interpretation of the financial behavior of individuals and institutions in terms of a theory of portfolio choice, relating sector requirements and preferences to the properties (such as risk, quality, and the like) of the available assets and debts; second, so far as over-all financial markets are concerned, emphasis on the requirement of simultaneous equilibrium in the balance sheets of all individuals and institutions in the economy.

7. *The SEC's Report of Special Study of Securities Markets.*

This major report, released in mid-1963, resulted from the request of Congress that the SEC conduct a broad study of the rules, practices, and problems in the securities industry and of the adequacy of investor protection. The report was also concerned with an evaluation of the theories and mechanics of direct government regulation and industry self-regulation.

The report as released contains thirteen chapters. Chapter I sets forth general data highlighting the growth of the securities industry. Chapters II and III deal with the persons and business entities in the securities business, the standards and control relating to their entry into and removal from the business, and their activities and responsibilities. Chapter IV covers the primary and secondary distribution of securities.

In Chapters V, VI, VII, and VIII the Special Study explores the functions, structures, and problems of the markets in which securities are traded after initial distribution. This covers the exchange markets and the functions and activities of specialists, odd-lot brokers, and floor traders, as well as short selling and commission rate structure. It discusses the over-the-counter markets, both wholesale and retail, and quotation systems. It examines the various interrelationships among trading markets, including institutional participation in various markets.

Chapter IX contrasts the reporting and other requirements for listed securities with the near absence of similar protective provisions for over-the-counter securities. Chapter X deals with the purposes, effects, and enforcement of securities credit and margin regulations. Chapter XI is concerned with certain aspects of mutual funds not covered by the recent study conducted for the SEC by the Wharton School. It also contains the results of an investor survey and deals with selling practices, contractual plans, and portfolio transactions. Chapter XII discusses the self-regulatory pattern which is largely unique to the securities industry. Chapter XIII reports on the study of the May 1962 market break. A summary volume is also being prepared bringing together all the conclusions and recommendations set forth in the several chapters.

8. *Wharton School, University of Pennsylvania.*

The Securities Research Unit of the Wharton School is continuing its studies of securities markets, practices, and ownership. Previous analyses of mutual funds, the over-the-counter securities markets, and stock ownership are being carried forward as well as related studies. Of particular interest is the updating of over-the-counter markets study, financed by the National Association of Securities Dealers, and the intensive work being done on stock ownership. In the latter, financed by the Ford Foundation, investment preferences and trading characteristics of different groups in the population are being analyzed in detail. Also of importance is the study in progress of investment banking and the new-issue market, financed by the Investment Bankers Association of America. In addition, the Consumer Expenditures Unit is continuing its studies of saving behavior both in the United States and other countries.

9. *University of Chicago Stock Market Study.*

Under the auspices of the Center for Research in Security Prices, directed by Professor James H. Lorie and Lawrence Fisher, and sponsored in large part by a grant from Merrill Lynch, Pierce, Fenner, and Smith, the Center is engaged in large-scale research on stock prices. The general objectives are to determine the rates of return on listed common stocks for a number of holding periods since the mid-1920's, and further to determine the relationship between stock prices, on the one hand, and earnings, dividends, and other variables, on the other. The first report on the project's findings appeared in the January 1964 issue of the *Journal of Business.*

10. *Brookings Institution Research in Capital Markets.*

Publications of the Brookings Institution in this area have included the basic work of Gurley and Shaw, the studies of W.

H. White on the influence of the interest rate on investment planning, and the recent volume by Ott and Meltzer on the issue of federal taxation of municipal securities. Work is expected to continue at Brookings on these and related subjects.

11. The NBER's Corporate Bond Research Project.

This project was completed in 1960 with the publication of W. Braddock Hickman's *Statistical Measures of Corporate Bond Financing since 1900.* The three volumes that resulted from this study represent an exhaustive compilation of data on corporate bond financing for 1900–44 and an intensive analysis of their implications. The first volume presents and analyzes broad aggregate statistics on new bond offerings, extinguishments, outstandings, and defaults. The second volume is a study of the detailed characteristics of bond offerings and defaults and the experience record by quality classes. The third volume contains the underlying statistical data.

12. The National Bureau's Pension Fund Study.

Under the general direction of Roger F. Murray of Columbia University, this project was begun in 1958 under grants from the Maurice and Laura Falk Foundation and the LIAA. It is a study of the current and expected structure of pension funds and their impact on aggregate saving, the distribution of income, and the capital markets. The Forty-third Annual Report of the NBER contains a comprehensive progress report.

13. The NBER's Quality of Credit Study.

Under the general direction of James S. Earley of the University of Wisconsin, this project was begun in 1956 with a grant from the Merrill Foundation. An investigation of changes in the quality of credit encompassing a wide variety of credit channels and instruments, it includes work on the quality of bank credit, trade credit, corporate bonds, including convertible bonds and direct placements, residential and farm mortgages, and consumer credit. A progress report on the study as a whole is contained in the Forty-third Annual Report of the NBER.

14. The NBER's Study of Interest Rates.

Under the general direction of Joseph W. Conard and William H. Brown, Jr., of Swarthmore College, this project was begun in 1960 under a grant from the LIAA. It involves an intensive study of the behavior and the determinants of yields on financial assets in the United States, with emphasis on the period since 1951. A progress report is contained in the Forty-third Annual Report of the NBER.

15. The Wealth Inventory Planning Study.

Under the direction of John W. Kendrick at George Washington University, the Wealth Inventory Planning Study was established recently, with a grant from the Ford Foundation, to prepare proposals for a comprehensive benchmark inventory of national wealth. It is hoped that the benchmark estimates can eventually be worked into a form which would permit the continuous collection of balance-sheet and wealth estimates as part of the national economic accounts.

[The article concludes with a sixteen-page bibliography of financial research works.]